ADULT ONLY GOLF JOKES

Guaranteed to make you giggle!

HINKLER
BOOKS

Joke Compilation: Scribblers and Writers
Cover Design: Sam Grimmer
Illustrations: John Shakespeare
Editor: Jasmine Chan
Typesetting: Midland Typesetters, Maryborough, Vic, Australia

Adults Only Golf Jokes
First published in 2004 by Hinkler Books Pty Ltd
17-23 Redwood Drive
Dingley Victoria 3172 Australia
www.hinklerbooks.com.au

First printed in 2004
Reprinted 2005

ISBN 1 7412 1655 9

Printed and bound in Australia

INTRODUCTION

There's no greater location for jokes than the golf course. With its mixture of odd rules, strange equipment and crazy characters who are dedicated to playing one of the most confounding games in the world, it's the perfect source for humour.

And let's not forget the drink and the inter-action between the sexes!

Throw in God, St Peter and the Devil and you have the perfect combination for gags and jokes.

So enjoy our laugh-laden trip along the fairways, into the rough and out of the sand-traps, with our tribute to the great golf jokes.

CLASSIC GOLF GAGS

Two pals are about to tee off at the first.

One of them puts his ball down and is ready to hit, when his mate says, 'Hey, what's with the ball? It looks different to anything I've seen.'

His mate says, 'It sure is. It's changed my whole golf game. You see, you can't lose it.'

'What!'

'True. You can't lose it. If it goes into the rough, it changes into spectacular flashing rainbow colours—you can't miss it.'

'Wow!'

'And,' continues his mate, 'If it goes into the trees and scrub, it's got a little transmitter and it lets out a sound which you can follow and you find it.'

'That's amazing!'

'And, if it goes into the water, it floats on top of the surface until you come and get it. You can't lose it.'

'Fantastic. I must get one of those. Where did you get it?'

'I found it . . .'

A travelling salesman is in a new town and having finished his appointments by lunch-time, decides to fit in a round of golf at the local club.

He goes out there and is greeted by the pro at the shop, who welcomes him and organises the clubs.

The salesman says: 'Is there someone who can caddy for me? Seeing as I don't know the course, it would be good to have someone who knows his way around.'

'Knows his way around? Reg is the man for you. Reg learnt to play on this course; he's won 21 club championships and he knows every blade of grass. In fact, he knows every beetle hiding under every blade of grass.'

The salesman thinks this is pretty good, so he says, 'Okay, Reg it is, then.'

'You go to the first tee,' says the pro, 'and I will send Reg around. Of course, with all that experience you will find he is of a mature age these days, but he's still invaluable.'

The salesman goes to the first tee, does a few exercises, then looks around to see an old bloke heading towards him on a Zimmer frame. He's 90 years old.

'Mature age!' thinks the salesman. 'Oh, well, it might be a long afternoon, but at least he knows the course.'

They introduce themselves to each other, the salesman tees up and lets rip with his tee shot.

The ball slices beautifully and curves to the right. The salesman has lost it entirely.

'Reg, Reg,' he cries, 'did you see it?'

'Yep,' says Reg confidently.

'Where is it?'

There is a long silence and then Reg says, 'I forget . . .'

A golfer comes into the club house after a bad round. The pro says, 'It looks like it was a pretty rough day.'

The golfer replies, 'You bet it was. The best two balls I hit all day was when I was coming out of the sand trap and stepped on the rake!'

Joe was a moderately successful golfer, but as he got older he was increasingly hampered by incredible headaches.

His golf, personal hygiene and love life started to suffer, he

managed to push on, but when his game turned really sour he sought medical help.

After being referred from one specialist to another, he finally came across a doctor who solved the problem.

'The good news is I can cure your headaches,' said the doctor.

'But the bad news is that it will require castration. You have a very rare condition which causes your testicles to press up against the base of your spine. The pressure creates one hell of a headache. The only way to relieve the pressure and allow your swing to work again is to remove the testicles.'

Joe was shocked and depressed.

He wondered if he had anything to live for, but then figured at least he could play reasonable golf again.

He decided he had no choice but to go under the knife.

When he left the hospital, his mind was clear, but he felt like he was missing an important part of himself.

Nevertheless, as he walked down the street, the sun began to shine and he realised that he felt like a different person.

He made a vow to himself—he could make a new beginning, swing free and live a new life.

He went to the club for a drink and as he walked past the

pro shop, he thought, 'That's what I need—a new outfit.'

He entered the shop and told the salesman, 'I'd like some new golf slacks.'

The salesman eyed him briefly and said, 'Let's see, size 44 long.'

Joe laughed, 'That's right, how did you know?'

'It's my job.'

Joe tried on the slacks, they fitted perfectly.

As Joe admired himself in the mirror, the salesman asked, 'How about a new shirt, I've got some great new stock.'

Joe thought for a moment and then said, 'Sure.'

The salesman eyed Joe and said, 'Let's see, a 34 sleeve and a 16 neck.'

Joe was surprised. 'That's right, how did you know?'

'It's my job.'

Joe tried on the shirt and it fitted perfectly.

As Joe adjusted the collar in the mirror, the salesman asked, 'How about new shoes, we just got new stock with soft spikes.'

Joe was on a roll and agreed.

The salesman said, 'Let's see, 9 wide.'

Joe was astonished, 'That's right, how did you know?'

'It's my job.'

Joe tried on the shoes and they fitted perfectly.

Joe walked comfortably around the shop and the salesman asked, 'How about a new hat?'

Without hesitating, Joe said, 'Sure.'

The salesman eyed Joe's head and said, 'Let's see, 7 5/8.'

Joe was really impressed, 'That's right, how did you know?'

'It's my job.'

The hat fit perfectly.

Joe was feeling great, when the salesman asked, 'How about some new underwear? I've got some great new imported stock, with golf motifs on them. They not only feel great, but look great.'

Joe thought for a second and said, 'Yeah, sure.'

The salesman stepped back, eyed Joe's waist and said, 'Let's see, size 36.'

Joe laughed, 'No, I've worn size 34 since I was 18 years old.'

The salesman shook his head, 'No, you can't wear a size 34—every time you swing, it would press your testicles up against the base of your spine and give you one hell of a headache . . .'

A golfer is having a bad time of it. His game is getting worse and worse.

Soon he's so bad, that he's embarrassed to be seen playing.

He decides that he'll practise early in the morning so that nobody sees him and hopes to get better again fairly soon.

On the first morning he's quite nervous but he tees up the ball on the first tee and gives it a smack.

The ball slices viciously and flies over the golf club fence.

The golfer hears one bounce and nothing.

He's so depressed, he packs his stuff up and goes home.

The next day he decides to persevere and tees up early again.

Again he slices the ball over the fence but this time the ball narrowly misses a man walking his dog.

The golfer rushes over to the man, apologising as he goes.

'You were here and did the same thing yesterday weren't you?' the man asks the golfer.

'Yeah, I seem to have a problem with golf right now,' the golfer answers.

'Did you see where yesterday's ball ended up?' the dog owner asks.

'No,' says the golfer.

'Oh, it bounced off a lamp-post onto the main road, caused a car to skid into a mother pushing a pram and both the mother and baby were killed instantly.'

'That's terrible,' exclaims the golfer, 'What do you think I should do?'

'Try dropping your left shoulder . . .'

My wife asked me why I don't play golf with Dean anymore. I asked her, 'Would you continue to play with a guy who always gets drunk, loses so many balls other groups are always playing through, tells lousy jokes while you are trying to putt and generally offends everyone around him on the course?'

'Certainly not, dear,' she replied.

'Well, neither will he . . .'

My friend,' said St Peter to the recently deceased arriving at the Pearly Gates, 'You did lead an exemplary life on earth, but there is one instance of you taking the name of the Lord in vain! Would you care to tell us about it?'

'As I recall,' replied the new applicant, 'It was in 1965, on the last hole at Pinehurst. I only needed a par four to break 70 for the first time in my life.'

'Was your drive good?' asked St Peter, with increasing interest.

'Right down the middle. But when I got to my ball, it was plugged deep in a wet rut made by a drunk's golf cart.'

'Oh dear,' said St Peter, 'A real sucker! Is that when you . . .'

'No. I'm pretty good with a three iron. I played the ball close to my feet, caught the sweet spot and moved it right onto the green. But it bounced on a twig or something—it was a very windy day—and slid off the apron right under the steepest lip of the trap.'

'What a pity!' said St Peter consolingly, 'Then that must have been when . . .'

'No. I gritted my teeth, dug in with an open stance, swung a smooth outside arc and back spun a bucket's worth of sand up onto the green. When everything settled down, there was my ball, only 10 cm from the cup.'

'Jesus Christ!' shrieked St Peter, 'Don't tell me you choked on the putt!'

It was a sunny Saturday morning, the sun was shining and Murray was beginning his pre-shot routine, visualising his upcoming shot when a voice came over the clubhouse loudspeaker: 'Would the gentleman on the Ladies tee back up to the Men's tee, please!'

Murray was still deep in his routine, seemingly impervious to the interruption.

Again the announcement—'Would the MAN on the WOMEN'S tee kindly back up to the men's tee!'

Murray had had enough.

He broke his stance, lowered his driver back to the ground and shouted, 'Would the smart-arse announcer in the clubhouse kindly shut the hell up—and let me play my second shot . . .?'

The other day I was playing golf and I hit two of my best balls.

I stepped on a rake.

A young man who was also an avid golfer found himself with a few hours to spare one afternoon.

He figured if he hurried and played very fast, he could get in nine holes before he had to head home.

Just as he was about to tee off, an old gentleman shuffled onto the tee and asked if he could accompany the young man, as he was golfing alone.

Not being able to say no, he allowed the old gent to join him.

To his surprise the old man played fairly quickly.

He didn't hit the ball far, but plodded along consistently and didn't waste much time. Finally, they reached the ninth fairway and the young man found himself with a tough shot.

There was a large pine tree right in front of his ball—and directly between his ball and the green.

After several minutes of debating how to hit the shot the old man finally said, 'You know, when I was your age, I'd hit the ball right over that tree.'

With that challenge placed before him, the youngster swung hard, hit the ball up, right smack into the top of the tree trunk and it thudded back on the ground—not a foot from where it had originally stopped.

The old man offered one more comment, 'Of course, when I was your age that pine tree was only 3 feet tall.'

Two golfers were having a quiet beer at the nineteenth.

'My wife says that if I don't give up golf, she'll leave me,' says one, staring quietly into his beer.

'Gee, that's a bit rough, mate,' says his pal.

'Yeah, I'm really going to miss her . . .'

TEN TRUISMS ABOUT GOLF

1. The toughest part about this great and wonderful game is getting off the tee and into the hole . . .
2. As the man, known for his philosophical approach, said, 'I know I can play better than this; I just never have.'
3. In golf, you can do many great things, but there is one thing for sure—you drive for show and putt for dough.
4. Golf is the only game out of all the sports where the ball lies poorly and the players lie well.
5. Real golfers, whether they passed maths at school or not, know how to count over five, when they have a bad hole.
6. If there is any larceny in the man, don't worry, you can bet that golf will bring it out.
7. Real golfers don't cry when they line up their fourth putt.
8. It is truly written, that of all sports, golf is an easy game . . . it's just a bastard to play.
9. In golf as in life, preparation is important, but it's the follow through that makes the difference.
10. If you can score 3 on one hole, then 11 on the next and then still move onto the next without shooting yourself or running away from the course, then you can survive anything in life.

CELEBRITY GOLF

Stevie Wonder and Jack Nicklaus are in a bar. Nicklaus turns to Wonder and says, 'How is the singing career going?'

Stevie Wonder says, 'Not too bad, the latest album has gone into the top 10, so all in all, I think it's pretty good.

'So, how about you? How is the golf?'

Nicklaus replies, 'Not too bad, I am not winning as much as I used to but I'm still making a bit of money. I have some problems with my swing. But I think I have got that right now.'

Stevie Wonder says, 'I always find that when my swing goes wrong I need to stop playing for a while and think about it. Then the next time I play it seems to be all right.'

Jack Nicklaus says, 'You play golf!'

Stevie Wonder says, 'Yes, I have been playing for years.'

And Nicklaus says, 'But I thought you were blind, how can you play golf if you are blind?'

Stevie replies, 'I get my caddie to stand in the middle of the fairway and he calls to me. I listen for the sound of his voice and play the ball towards him, then when I get to where the ball lands, the caddie moves to the green or further down the fairway. Again, I play the ball towards his voice.'

'But how do you putt?'

'Well,' says Stevie, 'I get my caddie to lean down in front of the hole and call to me with his head on the ground and I just play the ball to the sound of his voice.'

Nicklaus says, 'What is your handicap?'

Stevie says, 'Well, I play off scratch.'

Nicklaus is incredulous and says to Stevie, 'We must play a game sometime.'

Wonder replies, 'Well, people don't take me seriously so I only play for money and I never play for less than $100,000 a hole.'

Nicklaus thinks it over and after concluding that his career is on the slide and a few hundred grand wouldn't go astray, he says, 'Okay, I'm up for that—when would you like to play?'

Stevie Wonder replies, 'I don't care; any night next week is okay with me.'

Jesus and Arnold Palmer were playing golf.
It's Arnold's turn to tee off and he does so.

It's a long drive straight up the fairway and he's about a five iron off the green.

'Not bad,' Jesus says.

Jesus steps up to tee off, but his drive slices badly and lands on an island in the middle of a water hazard.

Jesus calmly walks across the water to take his next shot.

'Jesus!' yells Palmer, 'Who do you think you are, Jack Nicklaus?'

CELEBRITY GOLF SLANG

Calista Flockhart	A shot that is a little short, but still pretty.
Kate Winslet	A shot that is a little bit fat, but otherwise beautiful.
Danny DeVito	Short, fat and ugly.
Michael Jackson	A ball that moonwalks—that is, hits the green and then backs up.
Monica	A putt that is all lip and no hole.
Stevie Wonder	To miss a very short putt.

Buddha	Simply beautiful.
Lawrence of Arabia	You have spent the day in the sand.
Burke & Wills	You'll need to dig that one out.

Tiger Woods, in need of a well-earned rest, flew off to Nepal.

But like any golfer on holiday, he simply had to try the local links—a mountainous course situated high in the Himalayas.

The club was delighted to welcome him, but disappointed that they couldn't provide a caddie, as the Sherpas who usually attended were all busy working on an Everest expedition.

However, the club assured him they could provide a yak who would serve very well instead.

'A yak?' said Tiger incredulously.

'Sahib Woods,' assured the secretary, 'He is well versed in the art of caddying. He knows all the rules, carries the bag easily, has plenty of local knowledge and can point the best way around the course and, of course, will not chatter incessantly. He is perfect.'

'Well, okay,' said Tiger.

'Can I just add, however, that although this animal is of inestimable value, you have to watch out for him as he has one little idiosyncratic habit—he likes to sit on golf balls.'

'What!' said Tiger.

'It is, however, no problem,' says the club manager, reassuringly. 'You just have to reach under him and remove the ball. The yak will then continue on with the caddying.'

Forewarned and only slightly perturbed, Tiger set out.

Over the first eight holes, he had only had to remove the ball from beneath the sitting yak twice.

Then on the ninth hole he had to drive the ball blind over a rocky outcrop.

The yak took off after it and Tiger followed the yak.

He caught up with it beyond the rocks. It was sitting in a water hazard—right up to its neck.

Tiger stripped off and dived in the icy water to rescue his ball.

He groped around under the yak but could not feel it at all.

He surfaced, took another deep breath and tried again.

Still nothing.

Almost frozen, he tried again but with the same result.

Finally he gave up and frozen to the bone, made his way back to the clubhouse.

'Hey fella, what's going on? I'm freezing and my round's ruined.'

He explained to the secretary how he had dived three times for his ball but that the yak refused to move.

He told the man how he couldn't find his ball and was almost frozen to death in the process.

'And,' he went on 'That bloody yak is still sitting out there in the water hazard.'

The secretary was very apologetic. 'A thousand apologies, Mr Tiger, sir. I forgot to tell you. The yak also likes to sit on fish . . .'

Q. Did you know that OJ Simpson, Monica Lewinsky, Ted Kennedy and President Bill Clinton are all avid golfers?

A. OJ's a slicer, Monica's a hooker, Ted Kennedy can't drive over water and Clinton can't seem to hit the right hole!

At Augusta, Bill Clinton is on the first tee.
A member approaches him and says, 'Mr President, I know that you are a most honoured guest here today. But even you must know that you cannot take your first shot 3 m ahead of the markers.'

Clinton ignores and prepares to take his shot.

The member tries again. 'Listen, Mr Clinton, I'm the Club Captain. I must remind you to go back to the whiter markers.'

Clinton looks up and says, 'There are three things to consider here. One, you are annoying me. Two, I've played here before and know all the rules. Three, this is my second shot. Now shut up and let me continue with my game . . .'

HAVE YOU HEARD ABOUT THE CELEBRITY GOLF TOURNAMENT?

OJ had a wicked slice.
Heidi Fleiss kept hooking.
Ted Kennedy had an affinity for water hazards.
Nobody would go to 'sudden death' with Jack Kervorkian.
Greg Louganis kept putting the ball in the wrong hole.
John Bobbitt couldn't get the ball in the air.
Monica Lewinsky kept 'lipping' the hole.

A t a pro-am, a celebrity golfer pulls out the putter and tries to run it across the rough, up a mound, down past the edge of the green, onto the green and into the hole—65 m all up.

One of the spectators says: 'Who does he think he is—God?'

Another spectator turns to him: 'Actually, that is God—he just thinks he's Greg Norman.'

A SHORT LESSON IN GOLF

So I went to see Jones, the golf pro at the local Golf Club, to ask him if he would teach me how to play.

He said, 'Sure, you've got balls, haven't you?'

I said, 'Yes, I certainly have, but sometimes on cold mornings they're kinda hard to find.'

'Bring them to the clubhouse tomorrow,' he said, 'And we will tee off.'

'What's tee off?' I asked.

He said, 'It's a golf term and we have to tee off in front of the clubhouse.'

'Not for me,' I said, 'You can tee off if you want to but I'll tee off behind the barn, somewhere.'

'No, no, a tee is a fine thing, about the size of your little finger.'

'Yeah, I've got one of those.'

'Well,' he said, 'you stick it in the ground and put your ball on top of it.'

I asked, 'Do you play golf sitting down? I always thought that you stood up and waddled around.'

'You do,' he said, 'You're standing up when you put your ball on the tee.'

Well, folks, I thought that was stretching things a little too far and I said so.

Then he asked me if I knew how to hold my club.

Well, after fifty years, I should have some sort of an idea and I told him so.

He said, 'You take your club in both hands.'

Folks, I knew right there and then he didn't know what he was talking about.

Then he said, 'You swing it over your shoulder.'

'No, no, that's not me, that's my brother, Big Bernie, you're thinking about.'

He asked me how I held my club and before I thought I said, 'In two fingers.'

He said that wasn't right and he got behind me and put both arms around me and told me to bend over, because he would show me how.

He couldn't catch me there, because I didn't put four years in the Navy for nothing.

He said, 'You hit the ball with your club and it will soar and soar.'

I said, 'I could well imagine.'

Then he said, 'And when you're on the green . . .'

'What's the green?' I asked.

'That's where the hole is,' he said.

'Sure you're not colour blind?' I asked.

'No, then you take your putter . . .'

'What's the putter?' I asked.

'That's the smallest club made,' he said.

That's what I've got, a putter.

'And with it,' he continued, 'You put your ball in the hole.'

I corrected, 'You mean the putter?'

He said, 'No, the ball. The hole isn't big enough for the ball and the putter too.'

Well, I've seen holes big enough for a horse and wagon.

Then he said, 'After you make the first hole, you go on to the next seventeen.'

He wasn't talking to me.

After two holes, I'm shot to hell.

Eighteen holes in one day?

'Hell, no, it takes me eighteen days to make one hole.

Besides, how do I know when I'm in the eighteenth hole?'
  He said, 'The flag will go up.'

CORPORATE GOLF

He went golfing with his boss. The boss hit his first drive 50 m and it lay 275 m from the cup, so he conceded the putt.

YOU KNOW THAT YOUR BOSS IS A GOLFER IF:

- He has a golf ball on a string, hanging from the rear vision mirror of his car.
- His daughter's wedding party was on the nineteenth hole of the golf course.
- He estimates a 'par' score for every task that he sets and awards 'eagles' or 'birdies' if you come in under budget . . .
- His local golf shop has his credit card number on file.
- He keeps a putter by his favourite chair to change the TV channels with.
- His pets are named 'Tiger' and 'JD'.
- The golf pro shop has a private line just for him.
- He sets staggered drive off times for all of his staff.
- He insists that you sign off on your card at the end of each day.
- Sometimes he varies the workload by having you work with a different partner.
- When he asks, 'What's your handicap?' he is not talking about your limp.
- He chooses his new car purely on the basis that his clubs fit easily in the boot.
- His kids know it is Saturday because his clubs are gone from the hall cupboard.
- When he is talking about a 'good lay', he is not referring to the office tart.

A young executive was asked by his boss to take some out of town visitors to a golf day.

The man was delighted, played 18 holes with the guests, had a few beers and laughs with the waiter in the clubhouse, said goodbye and then rushed home.

When he got home to tell his wife the good news, all was quiet.

He opened the bedroom door, alas, he found his wife in bed with his boss.

He left, went back to the course, into the bar and the waiter said, 'I thought you went home.'

The man explained, 'Yes, I went home, found my wife in bed with my boss, but as they were in the early stages I figured I may be able to fit in another nine'.

A t a posh club in Manila, a very arrogant and nasty American is playing a round with a client.

He is very abusive to his caddy but all smiles with his client.

At the sixth hole, 185 m over water, he demands of his caddy, 'What club do I use here?'

The caddy says, in broken English, 'When Mr Raymond Floyd play here last year, he use six iron.'

The golfer rudely grabs the six iron and hits the ball.

The ball lands in the middle of the pond and the golfer erupts, 'Hey stupid, you gave me a six iron and it was obviously not enough. I went right into the water!'

The caddy replies, 'That exactly what Mr Raymond Floyd did too.'

A barber was cutting hair one day, when a guy came into the shop with a bandage right in the middle of his forehead.

He put him in the chair and asked what happened.

The guy said, 'Yesterday I was playing golf with my mother in law. On the second hole, she sliced her ball way over into a cow-pasture. She really hates to lose a ball so we looked and we looked and we looked. But no matter how hard we looked, there was simply no ball in sight. Just an old ugly cow. My mother-in-law screamed, "I'm not leaving till I find that ball." After continuing the useless search, I passed by the cow and thought that I had nothing to lose, so I lifted the cow's tail and sure enough, there was a ball stuck in the cow's arse. I called my mother in law over and said, "Does this look like yours?" And she hit me in the head with a seven iron.'

A man of the cloth is invited to a big corporate day. He has never played golf before and is a bit nervous.

He lines up for the opening hole, a nice short par three.

He swings and hits a terrible shot. The ball fires off to the left, hits a tree, bounces onto a rock, clips a branch, plops on the green and as if guided by radar, careers across the green, hits the pin and drops in the hole.

He's scored a hole in one.

After all the back-slapping, he quietly looks up to heaven and says, 'Thankyou, Lord, but I'd much rather do it myself . . .'

An inter-office golf game was held every year between the Marketing Department and the Support Staff.

The Support Staff whipped the Marketing Department soundly.

To show just how the Marketing Department earns their keep, they posted this memo on the bulletin board after the game:

'The Marketing Department is pleased to announce that for the 2004 Golf Season, we came in 2nd place, having lost but one game all year. The Support Staff, however, had a rather dismal season, winning only one game.'

Four international executives—an American, a Britain, a German and a Japanese—are playing golf.

On the third hole, a ringing sound is heard.

The British golfer fumbles in his bag, picks out his cellular phone, turns away from his partners and has a brief conversation.

'Terribly sorry, chaps,' he says after the call, 'but one has to keep one's finger on the pulse and all that.'

His companions murmur acknowledgment.

On the fourth hole there is another ring.

The American says 'excuse me,' places his thumb to his ear and holds his pinkie near his mouth and has an intense conversation.

He turns back to the bewildered group.

'Oh,' he says, looking at their puzzled faces, 'this is the latest thing on the Coast. I've got a microphone grafted into my pinkie and a receiver in my thumb. It's really convenient.'

They play on for a few more holes, at which point there is a loud ring.

The German, who had been leaning over his putt, snaps to attention. 'Ja, verstehen, verstehen, ja, ja. Auf Wiedersehen.'

He snaps back to normal.

The other three are astounded.

'I vill explain,' he tells his playing partners.

'This is really the state of art. I haff the microphone grafted into my lower lip and the receiver grafted into my earlobe.

'All I have to do to answer the telephone is to straighten my neck.'

Everyone is impressed.

Finally, on the 18th hole, muted chimes are heard.

The Japanese businessman drops his clubs, blurts 'So sorry,' and runs into the bushes. Everyone waits.

After 15 minutes the American goes to check on his colleague.

He finds Mr Tanaka squatting, trousers around his ankles, eyes closed and grimacing. 'You okay, Tanaka-san?' he asks.

'Everything is fine,' Mr Tanaka replies. 'Just awaiting fax from home office.'

There was a guy in my office who was an avid golfer. He played golf every chance he got—in the rain, in the cold, he even used black balls to play when there was snow on the ground.

His wife joked, half in jest, that she was a golf widow and she really wouldn't miss her husband all that much if he died before her, for he was never around anyhow.

He spent all his spare money on golf items and gadgets—trick exploding balls, tees with no indentation on the top so the golf ball would roll off it, towels with witty golf sayings on them and all kinds of golf hats.

One night he was in bed asleep after having played 36-holes of golf that day.

He was tired, but he dreamed of replaying the whole round.

Suddenly his dream was interrupted by the appearance of an angel.

It was an angel like he had seen in biblical drawings and other art work depicting angels.

He was instantly awake.

The angel, with a full set of wings and wearing a long flowing white robe, stood at the foot of his bed. 'John,' the angel said.

'Yes, what is it? You are an angel, aren't you?' John asked.

'Of course I'm an angel. You don't think I'd normally walk around in this silly costume, do you? In fact, I'm your guardian angel,' the angel replied.

'Does that mean I get three wishes?' John asked.

'No, I'm not that kind of guardian angel,' the heavenly being answered.

'As you know, John, you're getting on in years and you don't have as much time left on earth as you once did.

'Although I can't grant wishes for you, I can answer questions you might have about the hereafter. You do believe in the hereafter, don't you, John?'

'Oh yes and I've been good, with maybe the possible exception of having played too much golf in my lifetime,' John replied.

'Playing golf is like going fishing,' replied the angel. 'There is no such thing as playing too much golf or going fishing too often. Do you have any questions about heaven?'

'As a matter of fact, I do,' answered John. 'I've often wondered if there are any golf courses in heaven. Can you answer that question for me?'

'John, no one has ever asked me that question before,' said the angel. 'I'll have to go back and check on it. Go back to sleep and I'll be back in about 20 minutes.'

With that, the angel disappeared. John rubbed his eyes and opened them again.

The angel was gone and John wondered if all that had happened or that he had just had a weird dream.

He rolled over on his side and was soon snoring softly again.

True to his word, the angel reappeared within 20 minutes. 'John,' the angel called.

John woke up to see the angel again standing at the foot of his bed. 'Oh, you're back.'

'Yes, John, I'm back and I have the answer to your question. But before I tell you, I have to advise that the answer is in two parts, good news and bad news. Which do you want first, the good news or the bad news?'

'Oh dear, I suppose give me the good news first,' responded John.

'Okay, the good news is there are golf courses in heaven. All the courses have been designed by Bobby Jones, Arnold Palmer and Jack Nicklaus. There are no greens fees and electric carts are provided at no charge. You have the choice of any brand of clubs you desire. Each course has 36-holes. The greens are always freshly mowed, the sand traps freshly raked, the roughs aren't too high and you never lose a ball in the water, for the balls float. When you hit a ball into the woods they always ricochet back into the middle of the fairway. And on every par three hole you will score a hole-in-one. Yes, you will have a wonderful time playing golf in heaven.'

'Oh, that sounds wonderful. With all that good news what could the bad news possibly be?' John wondered aloud.

'The bad news is you have a 9.30 tee off tomorrow morning . . .'

DICTIONARY OF GOLF

19th hole
The only hole on which golfers do not complain about the number of shots they took or a place where most golfers find their best lies.

Aardvark
There's an albatross, an eagle and a birdie, all for scoring, in varying degrees, under par on a hole. We'd like to introduce the aardvark. The aardvark sounds more like your score—absurd, almost beyond belief. It can be as many strokes over par as you care to nominate. 'At the fifth, I had an aardvark 11 . . .' Sounds good, huh?

Ace
To somehow complete a hole in a single stroke. The odds against this happening are said to be calculated at something of the order of 50,000 to one. So how you can claim you did it deliberately, especially as you had nine at the previous hole before you lost the ball, is beyond all good reason.

Addressing the ball
Talking to the ball before it is hit, 'Please, please, pleeeeeese! Just go straight, you little bastard, for once.'

Albatross
A double eagle or a score of three under par on a hole. Rarely employed as a tactic by the amateur golfer. See 'Aardvark'.

Approach shot

A shot which, if it had not gone into the water, would have swerved to the left and landed on the adjoining green or involuntarily struck the Club Manager's Volvo in the car park.

Army

Both the group of people that follow a particular golfer, i.e. Arnie's Army, or a phrase used to describe the inconsistent and erratic wayward shots of amateur golfers, that is, 'left-right, left-right . . .'

Away

The player whose ball lies farthest from the hole is 'away' and it is his turn to make the first putt. After the stroke is taken, if the ball still lies farthest from the hole, then perhaps you should take up ice hockey.

Back nine
The final 27 holes of an 18-hole golf course. Very character-building.

Backswing
The part of the swing that takes place after the ball has been improperly addressed but before it has been sent to the wrong destination. Requires skill.

Bag rat
Caddie. Is supposed to give you the club and advice, not lip . . .

Ball
A dimpled, sphere with a weight of 1.62 ounces and a diameter of 1.68 inches that will enter a cup 4.25 inches in diameter and 4.0 inches deep after an average of 3.87 putts, but for most golfers will not do what it is supposed to.

Banana Ball
A curvaceous slice, especially for those dogged with the birth defect of playing golf left-handed. For a right-hander, it is a ball that starts to the right and continues to curve right, until it nearly lands behind the golfer who hit it. For the leftie, the ball arcs beautifully left and usually lands 30 m forward and 55 m sideways. This shot is one reason why the word 'fore' is heard on the golf course, along with 'shit' and 'poop'.

Barky or Barker
When one of your shots strikes a tree and you still make par for the hole, you have made a barky or barker. Not recommended for that rare breed, the environmentalist golfer.

Beach
The bunkers and other sand-covered areas at a golf course are

known collectively as the beach, sometimes camel grass and they have brought many a good round to an early close and many a potential career to an abrupt finish.

Birdie
One under par, often called a Mulligan. It is also very often the best of one or more practice swings and a six metre 'gimme' putt.

Blow Up
To have your game come apart at the seams. Easily recognised: When your score is blowing up, so are you. Recognised by errant, bad behaviour, including throwing clubs, cursing in several languages, going red in the face and threatening to insert a five iron into the caddy.

Body Language
Nervous leaning movements, particularly while putting, to 'persuade' the ball to go in a desired direction. If the ball fails to do so, these movements are often followed by a series of vulgar gestures and physical expressions, which re-appear later after nine beers at the 19th.

Bogey
The number of strokes needed to finish a hole by a golfer of average skill and above-average honesty. A contentious score, known to cause disputes and break friendships. See also 'Double Bogey' and 'Aardvark'.

Boss of the Moss
A smart-arse title. A golfer who is especially proficient on the grassy green sward. Hacks need not apply.

Break
1. The shifting or changing of the direction of a putt caused

ADULTS ONLY GOLF JOKES • 31

by the slope or slant of a green.
2. The splitting of the shaft of the putter caused by the rage or wrath of a player.
3. The shattering of the spirit of said player.

Bunker

A hazard consisting of an area of ground along a fairway or adjacent to a green from which a large amount of soil has been removed and replaced with a cavern made of sand designed to trap golfers. Archaeologist digs over the years have unearthed fragments of old balls, broken clubs, deteriorating sponsors' caps and the remains of the occasional luckless caddy.

Caddy

Individual who carries bags for the player and assists the player in the playing of the course, based on local knowledge. Ideally, a caddy should possess the eyes of a big-game hunter, the strength of a footballer, the patience of a diplomat and the memory of a Mafia witness. Many are just little smart-arses who can play a lot better than you.

Can

The hole. The cup. The place to put your putts. See, that thing over there! When you sink a putt, you canned it. Later, in the bar, when you have scored 127 for 18, your playing cops a canning from your mates, too.

Carpet

The green. Soft, well-manicured fairways are also referred to as being 'like carpet'. Occasional resting place for the prone golfer when a late-breaking 60-footer rolls in the hole and the emotion of it all becomes too much.

Centre city

A tee shot that lands directly in the centre of the fairway has gone to Centre City. Most hackers' drives visit the Western Suburbs.

Clubface

The metal or wooden striking surface that is located on the front of a clubhead above the sole and between the toe and the heel. There is a specific point on every clubface called the 'sweet spot', which, when it connects with a ball, produces maximum accuracy and power as well as a solid, gratifying feeling of perfect contact. Most golfers have about the same success finding it as they do the G-spot . . . Hard to find, but on the rare occasion you do, it's like reaching Nirvana.

Clubhouse

Place where the rules are prominently posted and no one reads them until there is a dispute.

Committee

The duly authorised drafters of the rules. A group to be avoided at all costs.

Competition

Form of play clearly established in the rules. Death by a thousand cuts, especially for the novice competitor.

Course

Area of play strictly regulated under the rules. Try and stay on it.

Courtesy

Type of conduct specifically mandated by the rules. If you must scratch your balls, don't use a jumbo tee.

Crap
The said rules overseen by the said committee, who should be avoided at all cost.

Dawn patrol
The golfers who are the first to play each day, so named because they start their march around the course at sunrise. Particularly skilled at playing the first two holes in the dark, they spend the rest of the day haranguing people about their exploits.

Delay
Golfers are expected to play 'without undue delay'. The question of exactly what constitutes undue delay has been under intensive study for 30 years. Having a leak in the bushes, sinking a beer or reading *How I Play Golf* by Tiger Woods in between shots can all contribute to 'delay', but still not be considered 'undue'.

Digger
A golfer who takes a big divot with his iron shots. Sometimes the bloody sod goes further than the ball, provoking the cry from your playing partner, 'Play the divot!' Ignore him with dignity.

Divot
Colourful Scottish word for the piece of turf scooped from the ground in front of the ball in the course of an iron shot. In Scotland, depending on its size, a divot is referred to as a 'wee tuftie', 'peg o' sward', 'snatch of haugh', 'fine tussock', 'glen', 'firth', 'loch' and the biggest of them all, 'damned English divot' (anything larger than 3m). The professionals sweep the ball beautifully with a divot. Hackers dig for gold.

Dog track
Derogatory term for a golf course that is not well maintained. You land the ball in every hole but the right one . . .

Double bogey

Two strokes over par. Positive types will describe a seven on a par five as a combination birdie and eagle on the same hole.

Down and dirty

Playing the ball 'as it lies'. No rolling the ball over or sitting it up. The way the game is meant to be played; your score is meaningless unless you play it *down and dirty*.

Dress

Although clothes in a variety of styles are acceptable on a golf course, a few general pointers are worth keeping in mind when selecting an outfit:

- never let good taste or any idea of the right combination of colours enter into your selection
- the combination of colours should be visible to an individual with normal eye sight looking out the window of a spacecraft in orbit
- it should be made out of a fabric derived from a substance that was mined or refined rather than grown or raised
- it should jam radar
- it should be composed of no fewer than eight separate colours or shades and should bear a minimum of four distinct emblems, two of which are in foreign languages
- when scuffed, the shoes should require repainting or re-stuccoing rather than shining
- any hat should be identifiable as such only by its position on the wearer's head.

Drive

The initial shot on each hole, made with a special wood, the driver, on par four and par five holes and with shorter woods or irons on par three holes. Because the drive is so critical to the play of the hole, total concentration is essential and thus, if the shot is spoiled because of some audible disturbance inadvertently caused by another player on the tee, such as a pair of shoelace tips clicking together or the wind whistling through an onlooker's eyelashes, it is customary to take the shot again. A very handy option for those who are dogged with the banana ball syndrome.

Drive for show and putt for dough
'He who putts the best wins the most.' This timeless golf cliché is shown every Sunday afternoon on network television.

Dub
To mishit a shot badly, causing it to roll on the ground and come to a stop far short of its target. A *dubber* is the guy in the group ahead who takes fourteen shots to reach the green and still insists he's having fun. Perhaps his marriage needs attending to.

Duffer
A golfer whose actual score on any given hole is ordinarily more than twice his or her reported score. Rarely gains membership at St Andrews.

Eagle
Unusually low score on a hole achieved by a golfer with an exceptionally good drive and one or two exceptionally good follow-up shots or by a golfer with an exceptionally poor memory or lucky beyond all dreams.

Elephant's ass
A poorly struck shot that is higher than it is long. Has been known to burn out on re-entry.

Equipment
According to the rules of golf, equipment is 'anything that can be

thrown, broken, kicked, twisted, torn, crushed, shredded or mangled; or propelled, driven or directed, either under its own power or by means of a transfer of momentum, into underbrush, trees or other overgrown terrain; or over the edge of a natural or artificially elevated area; or below the surface of any body of water, whether moving or impounded'. People keep buying it.

Etiquette

The rules of behaviour in golf. There isn't room here for a complete list, but a few of the more important ones are:

- never put tees in your nose
- never sneeze into your glove
- never concede a chip shot
- never hold a ball for another player to hit
- never practise drives against a backboard
- never wear golf shoes to a dance.

Fade

1. (Right-handed golfers) A shot that curves from left to right.
2. (Left-handed golfers) A shot that curves from right to left.

Your chances of winning the E Grade Monthly Medal disappearing into the bushes.

Fan
To miss the ball completely. The air moves, but nothing else does. The silence after is deafening, followed by barely imperceptible snickering. Has been known to lead to mental breakdown.

Fat, hit it
To hit the ground behind the ball first so that the shot has no spin and does not achieve the desired distance. Results often resemble an *elephant's ass*. A shot to be avoided.

Fight
To struggle with a particular golfing flaw. If all your poor shots are slices, you're said to be *fighting* a slice. If all your misses are hooks, you're said to be *fighting* a hook. If you miss all your short putts, you're said to be *fighting* a bad putter. If your rounds resemble boxing matches, take up crochet.

Flat bellies
The younger, thinner golfers on the PGA tour, coined by golfing legend Lee Trevino. On the other hand, the *fat bellies* are all playing the Masters circuit now and making more money in one tournament than they did in their entire career.

Flub
A shot that is too weak to register on conventional scorekeeping equipment. Eat more cereal at breakfast.

Fluff
A shot in which the clubhead strikes the ground behind the ball before hitting it, causing it to dribble forward one or two

yards. Usually followed by the shaking of the head and muttering of dire threats.

Follow-through

The part of the swing that takes place after the ball has been hit, but before the club has been thrown into the nearby water hazard. Can be spectacular and result in an appearance before the committee.

Fore

The first of several four-letter words exchanged between golfers as one group of players hits balls toward another in front of them on the course. Another 'f' word is often substituted.

Four-ball

A match in which two pairs of players each play their better ball against the other. Additional golf matches include: best-ball, in which one player plays against the better ball of two or the best ball of three players; three-ball, in which three players play against one another, each playing his or her own ball; and no-ball, in which two, three or four players, all of whom have lost all their balls, go to the clubhouse and play gin rummy.

Four-jack

To take four putts on a hole. Makes perfect sense to a lot of people, but only tolerable for those who can drive the green on a par five.

Foursome

Four golfers playing a round together. Three golfers are a threesome and two form a twosome. Four ladies playing slowly are a 'gruesome'. Four men playing after a long lunch at the 19th hole are a 'fearsome'. A single attractive woman playing alone is a 'toothsome'. A husband and wife playing together are a 'quarrelsome'. A group of golfers who give advice while watching another group tee off is a 'meddlesome'. A single player with a large number of jokes is a 'tiresome'. And two younger men playing a fast, sub-par round are a 'loathsome'. And as for old geezers in those frigging electric carts, why don't they give it away and play bowls?

Fried egg
A ball buried in the sand, with a ring around it created on impact. Too many fried eggs will make you lose your appetite for the game.

Front nine
The first half of an 18-hole golf course. A golfer who, by the end of the 9th hole, has shot within a few strokes of par for 18 is entitled to skip the second half of the course and head directly for the 19th hole and drink vast quantities of alcohol.

Frosty
Nickname for the score of eight on a hole. Synonymous with snowman because the figure eight resembles a snowman and Frosty is the most famous snowman. A figure to be avoided.

Give
An agreement between two golfers with a shared fear of the short game to 'give' each other their next putt.

Grounder
A golf shot that never leaves the ground.

Grocery money
Winnings from a golf bet that the winner pledges to spend on food and drink or groceries, but which is usually spent at the nineteenth hole.

Grinder

A player whose only mission is to achieve the best score possible. A hard worker. A serious player. To be avoided at all costs.

Greens fees

The charge for playing a round of golf. The more strokes one takes to play a hole the better value for money.

Green

A roughly circular area of smooth, lush grass where one 'putts for dough'.

Golf

People get out of the house or office to escape frustration and stress to play a game that causes frustration and stress.

Golf holiday

A chance for a group of blokes to go into the country for a few days without their spouses and children so that they can drink, gamble and play a bit of golf. Sometimes it can be combined with a conference so that the holiday becomes a tax deduction. Some people would suggest that a 'golf holiday' is an oxymoron.

God squad

Name for the group of PGA tour players who hold prayer meetings at professional golf tournaments and who thank God when they win as he always prefers born again Christians to win tournaments.

Goer
A shot that goes much farther than normal for the club being used.

Golf bag
Portable container with compartments designed to hold clubs, balls and other golfing accessories including a flask for whisky.

Golf club
The basic golfing implement. Also, a social organisation built around a golf course which has a distinct hierarchy that can be discovered by examining the car parking spaces and their labels. See 'Committee' and be warned.

Golf lawyer
A player known for knowing and constantly citing the rules. He will try to take advantage of your lack of knowledge to better his own score, so be careful.

Golf widow
Non-playing wife of an obsessive golfer.

Jail
A place from which escape is nearly impossible. Particularly when you are still 320 m from the green on a par four and you have used up three shots.

Jelly legs
A disability that afflicts nervous golfers. Especially debilitating when putting or surveying the end of night bar bill.

Jerk
To pull a shot or putt left of the intended line. Also, a playing partner who pulls a shot or putt left of his intended line, but doesn't actually mean to.

Juicy

A lie in the rough where the ball is sitting atop the grass, offering a clean approach. Can be so attractive that the player tends to pin the ears back and go for it . . . and the ball is last seen heading for the car park.

Keeping score

Determines who wins the game after four or five hours of playing. Golf is the only game where the highest score loses, except maybe for the card game Misere.

Kick

The way the ball bounces, sometimes good and sometimes bad. Or what a golfer does to his golf buggy when he is angry because he hit a bad shot.

Knee-knocker

An important putt to the outcome of the game, in the three-to-four-foot range that makes the putter nervous.

Knife

The toughest club to hit—a one iron. The old adage goes that if lightning starts looming in the distance, hold your one iron aloft, because not even God can hit a one iron . . .

Launched

Term for a drive that takes off like a jet plane and flies like a bird.

Leak oil

What a golfer does as his game begins to fall apart, a situation which can begin as early as the first tee.

Legs

A ball is said to have 'legs' if it continues to roll after landing. If it has too many legs it rolls past the hole and if it has not enough legs it does not make it to the hole. Legs are the things that hang down from the daggy shorts of a weekend golfer.

Lie

The place where the ball comes to rest after being hit by a golfer. Also refers to the number of strokes it took to get to the hole, as reported by that golfer.

Liz Taylor

A shot that's a little fat but not bad. Do not confuse with a Roseanne, which is very fat and not okay.

Local rules

A set of regulations that the committee makes up themselves for their own course, so that the members minimise the faults in their own games.

Long and wrong

Description of a golfer who can hit the ball long distances but seldom in the right direction.

Looper

Caddie.

Lost ball

A missing ball. It is declared a lost ball if it cannot be found after 10 seconds (opponent) or 20 minutes (your own).

Meat and potatoes par four

A long, straightforward par four that is uncomplicated and easy to play. If all things go right . . .

Military golf

Having to march a long way, from side to side of the fairways, to retrieve balls hit in a game. 'Left, right. Left, right.'

Money player

The golfer who makes the shots he needs to make under pressure and wins the bets. Only professionals and red-hot amateurs need apply.

Move

The golf swing.

Muff

To mishit a shot.

Needle

Verbally teasing and taunting your opponents so that you put them off their game. Some go to water at the first hole.

Nuked

When you hit a shot that achieves the absolute maximum distance for that club.

OB

The abbreviation for the three most depressing words ever uttered on a golf course—'out of bounds.'

On fire

You're on fire when everything you do works out just well. Then, having left the practice net, you stride to the first tee . . .

Oscar Brown
Nickname used for out of bounds.

Overcook it
To hit a shot too hard.

Par
The score that you should aim to end up with at the end of the game. It almost never happens.

Penalty
Strokes added to a golfer's score for play in contravention of the rules. See 'Committee' . . .

Pencil hockey
When the scorekeeper fudges the score in his own favour. Naughty, naughty, naughty.

Pin
The little sticky on the green thing that you can just see from the tee and to where you should be aiming your ball. It's amazing how, in the course of working your way up the fairway, how often it goes out of your view.

Pipeline
The centre of the fairway, so named because an irrigation pipe often runs down it. Not usually a problem for most hacks . . .

Play it as it lies
One of the two fundamental dictates of golf.

Playing through
This is what we invite the group behind us to do so that they won't be waiting on the tee for 40 minutes while we locate our balls.

Pond ball
An old, beat-up ball that won't be much of a loss if it lands in the water. A seasoned hacker has 31 in his bag.

Practice green
A place where a golfer goes to get an idea of the lie and to make sure his balls go in the hole. Usually leaves it all behind when he hits the course.

Practice tee
The place where golfers go to work on their faults and to try and convert a nasty hook into a wicked slice. Takes time, but it works.

Pro
A golf fanatic who is wise enough to stop spending so much time on the course, neglecting his business and improving his own game and instead, spends time trying to improve his game but getting paid for the privilege and making it his business.

Pro shop
This is where the fount of all knowledge, the pro, hangs out. The temptations in this place are:
• buy more lessons
• buy more gear
• buy more equipment.

Pull
To hit a shot straight but to the left of the intended target. It happens a lot.

Putt
To hit a shot straight but to the left, the right, beyond, short of, over or around the intended target. A genuine putt actually goes in the hole.

Rainmaker
A shot that is hit so high it travels close to the clouds. Some of these have been known to burn out on re-entry.

Rake
To pull the ball back into the hole casually with your putter after missing a putt or the thing that lies in the bunker waiting for you to repair the damaged surface after you have taken many shots at escape. Step on it and it may well be the best pair of balls you will hit all day . . .

Reading the green
Getting down on your haunches to look at the green and to pretend that you are able to predict where the ball will roll if you hit it at a certain speed. Best to just aim for the hole and hope. Besides, is holding your putter up, like the pros, really going to help?

Recovery shot
A shot whose primary purpose is to get out of trouble—for the genuine hacker, usually every second shot . . .

Relaxation
What you initially set out to do by taking up the game of golf but what you never get once you become a golfer.

Reload
After a bad tee shot to tee up a second ball or what you do when you are at the nineteenth and order another beer.

Robbed
When a putt doesn't go as it should then the golfer says that he was robbed or when you go back to the car and the stereo has been nicked while you were out on the course. At least you

can't blame the caddy for that, because he has been right by your side snickering at you all day.

Roller coaster
Round of golf that has good and bad holes in it—like a roller coaster ride. Some have been known to hop off half way through.

Sandbagger
A golfer who falsely posts high scores in order to inflate his handicap and then pounces at the next competition, to score maximum points, win the medal and laugh all the way to the bar

Sand trap
A deep depression filled with sand which has the ability to induce deep depression.

Scrambler
A golfer who plays somewhat erratically but manages to salvage good scores from inconsistent play.

Scratch
A player who has a zero handicap or what you do after you have spent the day retrieving balls from the scrub.

Scratch player
A player with a handicap of zero; a par golfer; a rat; a louse; a stinker.

Scuff
A lousy shot that results from hitting the ground before hitting the ball.

Senior
An old bugger.

Set them up
Improve your lie in the fairway or what you ask the bartender to do with the beers at the end of the day.

Shag
To retrieve golf balls or go home and have sex with your partner after a good game.

Shag hag
Any container holding practice balls or the groupies who hang around the clubrooms.

Short hole
Any par three.

Short stick
The putter or your sitting member after a night in the clubrooms at the nineteenth hole.

Side
Each nine holes—front and back.

Slam-dunk
To putt or chip the ball into the hole with great force. Can be seen as a heroic charge at the ball or the result of sheer desperation. The cup has been known to move as far as 5 m back from one of these.

Slice
A shot that curves to the right and is the beginning of the Left, Right military syndrome, which will dog you for the rest of the day.

Slick
Term used to describe fast greens or the most garish golf outfit of the day.

Spin
The variety of spins applied to the ball to make it curve around obstacles, turn into the wind or stop dead where it lands or the lies told in the clubroom after the game.

Spraying
To be unpredictable in the manner and the direction you hit your balls or to take a pee behind a tree.

Stance
The proper positioning of the feet for a golf stroke.
    You must remember:

- head down over the ball
- feet apart, not too much, not too little
- feet facing where you wish to hit the ball
- left arm straight
- right elbow bent
- hips loose
- and more
- seemingly by the time you have the handle half way up your left nostril you're just about there.

Sticks
Your clubs. Or, things to throw at invading crows. Or, things your clubs have been reduced to after a particularly serious tantrum on the thirteenth.

Stroke
A forward movement of the club that is made with the intention of hitting and moving the ball or a medical condition suffered by elderly golfers who should have stayed home in bed.

Tap-in
The glorious moment in golf when you stride up and knock the ball—usually from about 10 cm or less—into the hole. This is an exhilarating moment, best done after you have lobbed a fantastic wedge in from 90 m, stone-dead up next to the hole and it requires only the tap-in. The tap-in is not such a good result when it is your fourth putt. Tap-ins, in this instance, have been known to fly angrily across the green and strike the caddy in the groin.

Texas wedge
Using a putter or another flat iron for a hefty punch shot out of the scrub. Great use for the one iron!

Top it
One of the worst things that can happen to the hack golfer, especially on the drive—the club skims across the top of the ball, just moving it forward a few metres. The wise caddy moves adroitly out of the way, in case he gets topped too.

Unbelievable!
The cry heard from the rank hacker when, by some sheer fluke, the ball does exactly what he wants it to do—flying unerringly towards the target like a beautiful bird. There are often variations of this heard across the course, including Un-bloody-believable.

Undertaker
Many a funeral operator has been called to pick up the body of a dedicated golfer who has either had a stroke through the stress of it all or collapsed with a smile on his face having scored that elusive albatross at the long par five.

Under the weather
That sickly feeling on an early Sunday morning, after a hefty night on the piss, when you look down to tee off at the first and see five balls in a pink haze. The worst case scenario is a quiet chuck behind the bushes at the fifth. Never mind, a cold lunchtime ale will fix things up.

Underwear
A valuable inclusion in the golfer's wardrobe, but they are not usually revealed to the public—unless a particularly good shot encourages the player to strip down and run around the green in glee. They do not necessarily have to be in the same outrageous gaudy colours and mismatched check patterns as the accompanying outer layers of clothing. See 'Clothes'.

Vardon, Harry
A really good golfer, like you will never be.

Venerable
The state in which the oldest member is regarded as being—recognised for his longevity, golfing prowess, gentlemanly manners and etiquette, his image only tarnished by the way he farts in his sleep when he is dozing in his favourite armchair in the member's lounge after one too many brandies.

Whack
The marvellous sound of the ball striking a nearby tree after a full-blooded drive and which is last seen rocketing at head height into the next fairway.

Water hazard
A magnet for the hacker's ball, lakes, rivers, creeks and dams are a nightmare for the nervous amateur. 'Don't hit in the water, don't hit in the water, don't hit in the water, don't hit in the water, don't hit in the water, don't hit in the water,' he repeats to himself over and over again. Splash.

X Factor
Some bastards just have it. That unerring ability to strike the ball beautiful, keep it in the middle of the fairway and knock it in the hole with two or sometimes one caress of the putter. All smiles, mark the card and move on. The rest of us have the Y Factor. As in, 'Why the hell did it go over there . . .?'

X-Ray vision
The great ability to find a seemingly lost ball in the rough. It's a sixth sense and if you've got it, cultivate it. It can save you thousands.

Yahoo

A wild thing on the golf course—loud clothes, loud style, loud mouth. Wants to bet you 20 bucks on every hole. Trouble is, he often has the talent to back it up. Avoid him at all costs.

Yachting

Almost as frustrating a game as golf.

Yips

A dreaded nervous condition, usually picked up by the pros or the serious amateur, when hovering over the putt, they get the shakes and can't control the stroke. The hacker usually gets the same feeling when reaching for the wallet to pay for his round of drinks at the nineteenth.

Zap

When lightning strikes the bag and melts the clubs, leaving the golfer with a permanent ringing in the ears and a need to urinate whenever the microwave goes off. Let's hope it does not happen to you.

Zero

The lowest number of Stableford points you can get—a very embarrassing moment and a pointer to you giving up the game and taking up bowls.

Zoo

The nineteenth about an hour before closing time . . .

COUNTRY GOLF COURSES

When he sat down at the table at the bush golf club where he was a guest, he noticed that the dishes were the dirtiest that he had ever seen in his life.

'Were these dishes ever washed?' he asked his waitress, running his fingers over the grit and grime.

She replied, 'Of course they were cleaned. They're as clean as soap and water could get them.'

He felt a bit apprehensive, but didn't wish to offend and they all started eating.

Indeed, the meal was delicious and he paid his compliments in spite of the dirty dishes.

When dinner was over, the hostess took the dishes outside and yells—'Here Soap! Here Water!'

YOU KNOW THAT YOU ARE AT A COUNTRY GOLF CLUB WHEN:

- They think a stock tip is advice about grooming your dogs.
- 'He needed killing' is a valid defence.
- A golfer and his dog use the same tree.
- The general idea of talking during sex is, 'Ain't no cars coming, baby.'
- The PC keyboard in the office only goes up to #6 board.
- The diploma on the wall says, 'From the Trucking Institute'.
- The barman thinks Dom Perignon is a Mafia leader.
- A 7 course meal is a bucket of KFC and a six pack.

- When asked, your partner says that Jack Daniels is on his list of 'Most Admired People'.
- They borrow dad's tractor for their first date.
- E-I-E-I-O is how you spell farm.
- The captain's beer can collection is considered a tourist attraction in your town.
- Going to the bathroom at night requires shoes and a flashlight.
- The travel agent thinks Genitalia is an Italian airline.
- Kids are regularly born on a pool table.
- They think safe sex is a padded headboard.
- Houses don't have curtains but your truck does.
- 'Loading the dishwasher' means taking your wife out and getting her drunk.
- The coffee table used to be a cable spool.
- The stereo speakers used to belong to the drive-in.
- The women have less teeth than the Halloween pumpkin.

Farmer George was not having a good day on the golf course. After he missed a 12" putt, his partner asked him what the problem was.

'It's the wife,' said George. 'As you know, she's taken up golf and since she's been playing, she's cut my sex down to once a week.'

'Well you should think yourself lucky,' said his partner.

'She's cut some of us out altogether!'

A man is driving down a country road to the golf club, when he spots a farmer standing in the middle of a huge field of grass.

He pulls the car over to the side of the road and notices that the farmer is just standing there, doing nothing, looking at nothing.

The man gets out of the car, walks all the way out to the farmer and asks him, 'Ah excuse me mister, but are you okay? Do you need any help?'

The farmer replies, 'I'm trying to win a Nobel Prize.'

'How would you do that?' asks the man, puzzled.

'Well, I heard they give the Nobel Prize . . . to people who are out standing in their field.'

INSTRUCTIONS POSTED AT A LOCAL GOLF CLUB

1. Back straight, knees bent, feet shoulder width apart.
2. Form a loose grip.
3. Keep your head down.
4. Avoid a quick back swing.
5. Stay out of the water.
6. Try not to hit anyone.
7. If you are taking too long, please let others go ahead of you.
8. Don't stand directly in front of others.
9. Quiet please while others are preparing to go.
10. Don't take extra strokes.

Very good. Now flush the urinal, go outside and tee off.

The local golf club is having a working bee and wood is needed to build a club house.

Some men in a pickup truck drove to a lumberyard.

One of the men walked into the office and said, 'We need some four-by-twos.'

The clerk asked, 'You mean two-by-fours, don't you?'

The man said, 'I'll go check,' and went back to the truck.

He returned shortly and said, 'Yeah, I meant two-by-four.'

'All right. How long do you need them?'

The customer paused for a moment and said, 'I'd better go check.'

After a while, he returned to the office and said, 'A long time. We're building a clubhouse . . .'

Jock, the green keeper, was out working on the greens when a barnstormer pilot landed on a nearby paddock.

The pilot walks over and says, 'I'll give you an airplane ride for £5.'

'Sorry, cannae afford it,' replied Jock.

'Tell you what,' said the pilot, 'I'll give you and your wife a free ride if you promise not to yell. Otherwise it'll be £10.'

Seeing a bargain, Jock went home and got his wife.

So up they went and the pilot rolled, looped, stalled and did all he could to scare Jock. Nothing worked and the defeated pilot finally landed the plane.

Turning around to the rear seat he said, 'Gotta hand it to you. For country folk you sure are brave!'

'Aye,' said Jock 'But ye nearly got me there when the wife fell oot!'

DEATH AND DESTRUCTION ON THE COURSE

James hit the ball long and hard, a magnificent swing but somehow something went wrong and a horrible slice resulted.

The ball went onto the adjoining fairway and hit a man full force.

He dropped!

James and his partner ran up to the stricken victim who lay, quite unconscious, with the ball between his feet.

'Good heavens,' exclaimed James, 'what shall I do?'

'Don't move him,' said his partner, 'if we leave him here, he becomes an immovable obstruction and you can either play the ball as it lies or drop it two club lengths away.'

This Aussie bloke had been saving for years for the ultimate golfing holiday and finally he was off.

He turns up at the Royal Nairobi Golf and Country Club looking forward to the best game of his life. He gets allocated a personal caddie.

He thought it a bit unusual that the caddie had a shotgun, but hey, what the heck.

Off to the first tee he goes but he's so excited that whack! the ball slices off into the deep bush.

'You'll be okay,' says his caddie as he heads off into the bush looking for his ball.

He goes in so deep and all of a sudden 'Whoom!'

Startled he turns around and sees the caddie with a huge smile on his face standing with one foot placed on this very dead lion.

'This is unbelievable,' he thinks and walks off to the next tee.

But, he's a little shaken and 'Thump!' the ball heads off into the deep bush again. 'You'll be right mate,' yells his caddie as once again he walks—this time with some trepidation—into the bush.

He turns quickly around and there's his caddie again—hugest smile ever on his face, his left foot placed on the head of a rhino.

'No worries!' yells the caddie and they complete the hole.

The Aussie is a little bit shaken as he stands on the next tee contemplating the water hazard in front of him and—would you believe it—he tops the ball into the water.

The caddie gives the thumbs up sign as he yells, 'You'll be able to get that, the water's pretty shallow.'

The Aussie is a little bit hesitant as he wades in and for good reason as out of nowhere a huge alligator surges through the water, grabs his left leg and rips it off.

Surrounded by blood red water, he yells to the caddie, 'Why didn't you shoot him?'

And the caddie yells back, 'Because you don't have a shot on this hole!'

Two couples play golf together regularly at their club. On the sixth hole, a par four, the second shot to the green must carry 80 yards over water.

For over a year, one of the women, Mrs Smith, could never carry the water and would always hit into it, totally psyched out by its presence.

Her friend in the group suggested that she might want to see a hypnotherapist as rumour was that such therapy could be of help in such a situation.

So the woman went to a hypnotherapist for four sessions.

In those sessions, the woman was hypnotised and the therapist would 'plant suggestions', so that when playing the second shot on the sixth hole, she would not see water, but rather a plush green fairway leading all the way up to the green.

About six months later, someone at the club asked whatever happened to Mrs Smith, as she hadn't seen her playing golf at the club for almost four months.

'It was terrible,' replies her informant, 'a few months ago, she drowned on the sixth . . .'

The first timer is unaware of the subtle nuances of the game and also of the etiquette.

He tears up the course, leaving a trail of destruction behind him—great chunks taken out of the turf. And that's just on the putting surface.

When he comes off, the clubhouse is abuzz with discussion about this maniac that has undone years of careful grooming of the course.

Because it's his first round, he is celebrating with a few pots and a huge meal in the dining room, when a quiet, discreet voice says, 'Excuse me, sir, but I'm the chairman of the Greens Committee.'

The new golfer looks up from his plate. 'Greens?' he says, pointing to his plate. 'Just the bloke I want to see. These Brussels Sprouts are bloody awful . . .'

The sailor and a priest were playing golf.

The sailor was not very good at it and uttered a loud 'Jesus, missed!' each time he missed.

The priest tolerated him for a few minutes and couldn't take it anymore.

'Do not blaspheme, my friend or God will punish you,' pleaded the priest.

It didn't make a difference, the sailor continued mouthing off, at the top of his voice, unabated.

One shot after another, the sailor played badly and followed up with 'Jesus, missed!'

Again, the priest said plaintively, 'Do not utter blasphemous words or God will show you a sign.'

It didn't help and the next stroke missed was followed by a loud 'Jesus, missed!'

A bolt of lightning dropped out of the clouds and struck the priest dead.

There was silence, followed by a voice heard in the clouds, 'Jesus, missed!'

We have it on good authority that the greatest causes of heart attacks for male golfers over 60 are female golfers under 30.

A young man playing by himself on a gorgeous clear morning, thinking he wouldn't be dead for quids.

After parring the first two holes, he lines up on the third, a 400 m par four and hits a screamer down the middle.

He lines up his second with a three iron, but shanks it.

It hits a tree, ricochets back, hits him between the eyes and he drops dead on the fairway.

His spirit floats up to the Pearly Gates.

'Who are you? says St Peter.

'Henry Chapman,' says Henry Chapman.

St Peter looks at his clipboard and scratches his head. 'I've got no record of you being due; how did you get here?'

'In two.'

The day he got a hole in one, I saw the state he was in when he got home.

He roared into the driveway, clipped the tree, tore up the garden, ran over one of the kids' bikes, injured the cat, sent the dog into a tail-spin, knocked over the fence and smashed into the garage door.

Mind you, it could have been worse.

Can you imagine the damage he would have done if he had been driving the bloody car . . .?

It was their second weekend of playing the great game, for the two long-time women friends.

One of them closed her eyes, took an almighty swing and hooked the ball to the right.

The club flew straight out of her hands, ricocheted off two trees and killed a pigeon in mid-flight.

Meanwhile, the ball continued on its merry way, bouncing off a sprinkler, hitting another golfer on the head, plopping on the green, then rolling majestically across the turf, where it neatly dropped into the cup for a hole in one.

The other woman looked at her coldly.

'Joyce,' she said archly . 'You are a sneak. You've been practising!'

DEVOTION

A couple had been happily married for 15 years. During this blissful existence, there was only one thing that Ruthie had forbidden her husband to do.

That was to open a small silver box, kept up on her dresser.

One day the husband was cleaning the mirror above Ruthie's dresser and accidentally knocked the silver box to the floor.

Out spilled six golf balls and a thick wad of cash.

The husband was bemused.

He counted the cash, which totalled $25,000.

Shocked but controlled, he put it all back.

At dinner he apologised to Ruthie for accidentally knocking the silver box to the floor.

'But, darling, I don't understand, what does it all mean?' he said.

He looked so sad and upset, Ruthie couldn't help it. She broke down and told him the truth.

Ruthie said that each time she cheated on him she put a golf ball into the box.

He thought about this for a while and figured, that wasn't too bad.

'We have been through good times and bad, Ruthie,' he said. 'Six times you drifted from the straight and narrow in 15 years. Naturally I'm disappointed, but I love you Ruthie and I can forgive that.'

'Oh, thankyou, thankyou, darling!'

'But the cash?' he said. 'Where did all the cash come from?'

Ruthie replied, 'Oh the cash!? You see my dear, each time I had a dozen golf balls I sold them for $10.'

A man and woman are sitting at the breakfast table. She is having a cup of coffee, he is reading the newspaper.

Wife to husband, 'Honey, if I die before you, will you remarry?'

Husband, quietly putting paper down, is a little surprised and replies: 'Well, we have had a good marriage and marriage is a good institution, so, yes, I would probably remarry.'

He goes back to reading the paper; she gets another cup of coffee and, after a few minutes, asks, 'Honey, if I die before you and you remarry, would you bring her to live in our house?'

He lowers the paper slowly, thinks for a second and says, 'Well, we worked hard to pay off the mortgage and it would be silly to move someplace else so, yes, I think I would bring her to live here.'

He returns to his paper, a few minutes passes and she asks, 'Honey, if I die before you and you remarry and you bring her to live here in our house, would you let her use my golf clubs?'

'Don't be ridiculous,' he says as he slams down the paper, 'she's a lefty . . .'

'Mildred, shut up,' cried the golfer at his nagging wife, 'Just shut up or you'll *drive* me out of my mind.'

'That,' said Mildred, 'wouldn't be a *drive*; it would be a short putt.'

A couple has a whirlwind, 30 day romance and even though they don't know too much about each other, they decide to get married.

After a couple weeks, the husband says, 'Honey, I have something I have to tell you. I'm a golf fanatic and I must play every day.'

'I also need to tell you something,' she replies. 'I'm a hooker and I need to do it every day.'

'That's okay,' he said, 'we'll just play dog-leg lefts.'

She: 'Let me get this straight. The less I hit the ball, the better I am doing.'

He: 'That's right.'

She: 'Then why hit it at all?'

An Englishman waiting to tee-off sees a funeral procession going by. It was a strange looking affair. The casket and the pall bearers were led by a man who had a dog by a leash and the rest of the people were walking in a straight line behind the casket.

Unable to resist his curiosity, he goes up to the man with the dog and asks, 'Excuse me for troubling you on such a sad occasion, but I have never seen such a strange funeral, the dog and all the people walking in a straight line?'

The man with the dog answers, 'This is my wife's funeral.'

'But why the dog?' asks the Englishman.

'She died because this dog here bit her,' said the man with the dog.

'Very sorry to hear that. Say, would you mind if I borrow the dog for a while?'

'Sure,' says the man with the dog, 'Get to the back of the line.'

The room was full of pregnant women and their partners. The Lamaze class was in full swing.

The instructor was teaching the women how to breathe properly, along with informing the men how to give the necessary assurances at this stage of the plan.

The teacher then announced, 'Ladies, exercise is good for you. Walking is especially beneficial. And, gentlemen, it wouldn't hurt you to take the time to go walking with your partner!'

The room really got quiet. Finally, a man in the middle of the group raised his hand.

'Yes?' replied the teacher.

'Is it all right if she carries a golf bag while we walk?'

A couple whose passion had waned saw a marriage counsellor and went through a number of appointments that brought little success.

Suddenly at one session the counsellor grabbed the wife and kissed her passionately. 'There,' he said to the husband, 'That's what she needs every Monday, Wednesday, Saturday and Sunday.'

'Well,' replied the husband, 'I can bring her in on Mondays and Wednesdays, but Saturdays and Sundays are my golf days.'

A fter an enjoyable eighteen holes of golf, a man stopped in a bar for a beer before heading home.

There he struck up a conversation with a ravishing young beauty.

They had a couple of drinks, liked each other and soon she invited him over to her apartment.

For two hours they made mad, passionate love.

On the way home, the man's conscience started bothering him something awful. He loved his wife and didn't want this unplanned indiscretion to ruin their relationship, so he decided the only thing to do was come clean.

'Honey,' he said when he got home, 'I have a confession to make. After I played golf today, I stopped by the bar for a beer, met a beautiful woman, went back to her apartment and made mad passionate love to her for two hours. I'm sorry, it won't ever happen again and I hope you'll forgive me.'

His wife scowled at him and said, 'Don't lie to me, you sorry scumbag! You played 36 holes, didn't you?'

I hear Maggie and yourself settled all differences, stopped fighting and decided to get married after all,' Jock said to Sandy, as they strolled towards the fifteenth.

'Seems the practical solution,' said Sandy. 'She's put on so much weight that we couldn't get the engagement ring off her finger . . .'

J ock and his nephew had spent a beautiful day on the golf course and were having a few drinks together in the clubrooms when the nephew confided in him, 'I have my choice of two women,' he said, 'A beautiful, penniless young girl whom I love dearly and a rich old widow whom I can't stand.'

'Follow your heart; marry the girl you love,' Jock counselled.

'Very well, Uncle Jock,' said the nephew, 'That's sound advice.'

'By the way,' asked Jock, 'Where does the widow live?'

THE 15 NATURAL LAWS OF GOLF

Simply appreciate these for what they are and your game will go into a whole new dimension. And you will be able to go into a rest home for the befuddled golfer.

Law 1
Yea verily, no matter how lousy your last shot was, the worst is yet to come. This law is in effect not only over the course of a hole, a round, a competition and a summer, but, eventually, a lifetime. It will dog you forever.

Law 2
It is truly written, your best hole in golf will be immediately followed by your worst hole.

Law 3
Law 2 applies also to your best round of golf. It will be reprised almost immediately by the most damning, ugly, nasty, soul-destroying 18 holes ever. The probability of the latter increases with the number of mates you tell about the former.

Law 4
The shorter the hole, the greater the red-faced embarrassment it will cause you. Do not attempt a par three of less than 100 m.

Law 5
Brand new golf balls have a high water attraction factor. The

mathematical theory is that the more expensive the golf ball, the greater its attraction to water.

Law 6
Golf balls never bounce off trees back into play. If one does, the tree is breaking a natural law and will probably be cut down by the next time you play.

Law 7
Tussocks devour golf balls.

Law 8
While appearing innocent and inert, sand is actually a living organism with an adherence factor that ensures you will never get it out of its clutches, even with five mighty blows with the wedge.

Law 9
The driver is a club possessed by the devil, with a particular propensity to curve the ball on the adjacent fairway.

Law 10
While a severe slice is a thing of awesome power and beauty, it will destroy you, your game and possibly your marriage.

Law 11
The higher a golfer's handicap, the more qualified he deems himself as an instructor. He usually starts on you at about the fourth hole, beginning with the classic line, 'Look, I don't want to tell you how to play the game, but . . .'

Law 12
According to the Keynesian theory of economics, the more money you spend on clubs and lessons, the worse your game will get.

Law 13

The more money you spend on golf attire, the worse your games gets and the louder the sniggering when you inadvertently wear it to a party.

Law 14

The length of the late-breaking putt that dropped on the seventeenth increases in proportion to the number of beers consumed later at the nineteenth.

Law 15

The number of fatalities on a golf course is directly proportional to the amount of alcohol consumed and the size of the fleet of golf carts on the course at the time.

GOD AND THE DEVIL

A keen but unskilled golfer plays the same course every week and has particular trouble with the water trap on the fourteenth hole. He loses a ball in it every time he plays that hole.

One round he decides that this process is too expensive and decides to use an old cut-up ball instead of a good ball.

He opens his bag and gets the old ball, tees it up and addresses it.

Just as he commences his backswing, a mighty voice comes from on high, 'USE THE NEW BALL . . .'

Figuring any advice from such a source should be worth following, he picks up the old ball and tees up the new one again.

He starts his backswing, but once again is interrupted by a voice from the sky, 'TAKE A PRACTICE SWING.'

The man steps away from the ball and rehearses his swing. Just as he steps forward to readdress the ball, the voice speaks again, 'USE THE OLD BALL.'

A n enthusiast was trying to learn golf and having a terrible time of it.

'I'd give just about anything to get this right!' he says aloud.

Straight on, the Devil appears and says, 'Anything?'

'Well, short of selling my soul, yes.'

'How about giving up sex for the rest of your life?'

'Done and done!'

He finishes the game in rare good form and rumour of his deal spreads through the clubhouse.

One of the members, a reporter, sees a story here and asks him, 'Sir, is it true you made a deal with the Devil to become a great golfer?'

'True, enough.'

'And you gave up sex as your part of the bargain?'

'True again!'

'And may I have your name, sir?'

'Certainly, it's Father Mike O'Ryan.'

SEX AND GOLF

A man was stranded on a desert island for ten years.
One day a beautiful girl swam to shore in a wet suit.

Man: 'Hi! Am I ever happy to see you!'

Girl: 'Hi! It seems like you've been here a long time. How long has it been since you've had a cigarette?'

Man: 'It's been ten years!'

With this information, the girl unzipped a slot on the arm of her wet suit and gave the man a cigarette.

Man: 'Oh thank you so much!'

Girl: 'So tell me how long it's been since you had a drink?'

Man: 'It's been ten years, too.'

The girl unzipped a little longer zipper on her wet suit and came out with a flask of whiskey. She gave the man a drink.

Man: 'Oh, thank you so much. That tastes like liquid gold. I can't believe this is happening to me. You are like a miracle'!

Finally the girl started to unzip the front of her wet suit and asked the man, 'So tell me then, how long has it been since you played around?'

The man looked at her and said excitedly, 'Oh, my God, don't tell me you've got a set of golf clubs in there too?'

A man went to a strange town to be the guest speaker at a business meeting.

When he arrived at his motel, he found he had a lot of time before the meeting so he got the directions for a nearby golf course from the clerk.

While playing on the front nine, he thought over his impending speech and became confused as to where he was on the course.

Looking around, he saw a lady playing ahead of him. He walked up to her, explained the situation and asked her if she knew what hole he was playing.

She replied, 'I'm on the seventh hole and you are a hole behind me, so you must be on the sixth hole.'

He thanked her and went back to his golf.

On the back nine the same thing happened and he approached her again with the same request.

She said, 'Well, I'm on the fourteenth and you are a hole behind me, so you must be on the thirteenth.'

Once again he thanked her and returned to his play. He finished his round and went into the club house where he saw the lady sitting at the end of the bar.

He asked the bartender if he knew the lady. The bartender said that she was a sales lady and played the course often.

So the bloke approached her and said, 'Let me buy you a drink in appreciation for your help. I understand you are in the sales profession. I'm in sales also. What do you sell?'

She replied, 'If I told you, you would only laugh.'

'No I wouldn't.'

'Well if you must know,' she answered, 'I sell sanitary towels.'

And the bloke started laughing.

She said, 'See I knew you would laugh.'

'That's not what I'm laughing at,' he replied, 'I'm a toilet paper salesman, so I'm still a hole behind you!'

Seamus O'Malley is playing golf when he takes a hard struck golf ball right in the crotch.

Writhing in agony, he falls to the ground. As soon as he can manage, he takes himself to Doctor O'Connor.

'How bad is it doctor?' asks O'Malley, 'I'm going on my honeymoon next week and my girlfriend is a virgin in every way.'

'I'll have to put your penis in a splint, Seamus, to let it heal and keep it straight. Sure, it'll be fine by next week.'

The doctor takes four tongue compressors and forms a neat little four-sided bandage and wires it all together

'An impressive work of art,' says the good doctor.

Seamus says nothing of this to his girlfriend, marries and goes off on his honeymoon.

That night in the hotel room she rips off her blouse to reveal a gorgeous set of breasts, a sight Seamus has not seen before.

'You're the first, Seamus. No one has ever touched these breasts.'

Seamus promptly drops his pants and replies, 'Would you look at this Brigid—it's still in the crate!'

There was a young lady golfer named Duff.
With a lovely, luxuriant muff.
In his haste to get in her,
One eager beginner
Lost both his balls in the rough.

A husband and wife love to golf together, but neither of them is playing as well as they want to, so they decide to take private lessons.

The husband has his lesson first.

After the pro sees his swing, he says, 'No, no, no. You are

gripping the club way too hard!'

'Well, what should I do?' asks the man.

'Hold the club gently,' the pro replies, 'just like you'd hold your wife's breast.'

The man takes the advice, takes a swing and POW!

He hits the ball 250 m straight down the fairway.

The next day the wife goes for her lesson.

After the pro watches her swing, he says, 'No, no, no. You're gripping the club way too hard.'

'What can I do?' asks the wife.

'Hold the club gently, just like you'd hold your husband's penis.'

The wife listens carefully to the pro's advice, takes a swing and THUMP.

The ball goes straight down the fairway, about 280 m.

'That was great,' the pro says. 'Now, this time, how about you take the club out of your mouth . . .'

There was a young golfer named Lear
Who went to jail for a year
For an act quite obscene,
On the very first green,
Under a sign saying 'Enter course here'.

Peter was not feeling well, bad enough that his wife Sharon had to go and get the test results from the doctor.

'Now Sharon,' says the doctor, 'I don't exactly know what the problem is—Peter may even die if he doesn't get the right treatment. The only thing is the right treatment is going to seem a little strange. Peter needs to golf as often as he has strength and you need to give him all the sex he can handle.'

Sharon nodded and left.

When she got home, Peter was anxious to find out what his test results were.

'Well Sharon, what did the Doctor have to say?'

Sharon looked him straight in the face. 'You're going to die . . .'

Q: What's the difference between a golf ball and a woman's G spot?

A: A guy will take 20 minutes to look for a golf ball.

Q: Why do they call it 'golf'?

A: All the good four-letter words were taken.

A blonde is out playing golf one sunny day, when she suddenly screams and runs back to the club house.

She approaches the resident pro and tells him, 'I've just been stung by a bee!'

'Where were you stung?' asks the pro.

'Between the first and second holes,' she replies.

'I'm not surprised,' answers the pro. 'Your stance is far too wide.'

One fine day in Ireland, a guy is out golfing and gets up to the sixteenth hole.

He tees up and cranks one.

Unfortunately, it goes into the woods on the side of the fairway.

He goes looking for his ball and comes across this little guy with this huge knot on his head and the golf ball lying right beside him.

'Goodness,' says the golfer, then proceeds to revive the poor little guy.

Upon awakening, the little guy says, 'Well, you caught me fair and square. I am a leprechaun. I will grant you three wishes.'

The man says, 'I can't take anything from you, I'm just glad I didn't hurt you too badly,' and walks away.

Watching the golfer depart, the leprechaun says, 'Well, he was a nice enough guy and he did catch me, so I have to do something for him. I'll give him the three things that I would want. I'll give him unlimited money, a great golf game and a great sex life.'

A year goes past and the same golfer is out golfing on the same course at the sixteenth hole.

He gets up and hits one into the same woods and goes off looking for his ball.

When he finds the ball he sees the same little guy and asks how he is doing.

The leprechaun says, 'I'm fine. And might I ask how your golf game is?'

The golfer says, 'It's great! I hit under par every time.'

'I did that for you,' responds the leprechaun.

'And might I ask how your money is holding out?'

The golfer says, 'That's the amazing thing, every time I put my hand in my pocket, I pull out a hundred pound note.'

The leprechaun smiles and says, 'I did that for you. And, finally, might I ask how your sex life is?'

Now the golfer looks at him a little shyly and says, 'Well, maybe once or twice a week.'

Floored the leprechaun stammers, 'Once or twice a week?'

The golfer looks at him sheepishly and says, 'Well, that's not too bad for a Catholic priest in a small parish . . .'

A puzzled golfer watched a fellow member don some very unorthodox gear in the clubroom.

'How long have you been wearing a corset?' he asked.

'Ever since my wife found it in the car,' was the reply.

An Australian professional went over to Japan to play in an important tournament. He took his younger brother as a caddy.

The first night in Tokyo, the golfer had to have an early bedtime but the brother decided to go out on the town. It was his first trip overseas, so he wanted to see what the big outside world was like.

He finished up in a house of ill repute and while he was having his wicked way with one of the young ladies, heard her scream, 'YAKAMOTO! YAKAMOTO!' She nearly brought the house down with it.

Assured in his mind and ego that this heartfelt cry of 'YAKAMOTO,' was an expression of satisfaction at his manhood, the brother returned to his hotel well satisfied with his night out.

The next day on the very tight course, his brother, the pro, is ready to tackle the difficult 187 metre, all-water carry, par three fifth hole. A proposition made even more difficult by the sudden arrival of a typical Japanese industrial smog.

He sees a flag in the distance, pulls out a four iron and drills it as straight as a gun barrel into what he thinks is the fifth green.

It lands on the grass and goes straight into the hole!

The crowd all rose as one and scream, 'YAKAMOTO! YAKAMOTO!'

The caddy brother says to his pro brother, 'From my limited understanding of Japanese, big brother, I think that means it was a great shot and you've hit the target.' To which the more experienced pro brother replied, 'Fraid not, little brother. I've aimed at the wrong green. YAKAMOTO, in Japanese, means wrong hole . . .'

A golfer named Sandy MacFarr
Went to bed with a Hollywood star
When he first saw her gash he
Cried, 'Quick, goot muh mashie!
Uh thunk uh c'n muk it in par.'

There was this golfer just starting out on the tour.
During his first match, in which he was going well, he spots this beautiful woman watching his every move.

He thinks to himself, 'If I play my cards right I could take her back to the motel.'

So, at the end of the round, he successfully woos her back to his room, where they make passionate and imaginative love.

When he finishes, he gets out of bed. She says, 'Where are you going?'

He says 'I'm going to ring up room service and get a bottle of champagne.'

She says, 'Jack Nicklaus would never leave a girl after he's made love to her once—get back into bed.'

So they go for it a second time.

When he's finished, he gets out of bed.

'Where are you going?' she asks.

'I'm going to ring up room service and get a bottle of champagne,' he says. She says, 'Jack Nicklaus would never leave a girl after he's made love to her twice—get back into bed!'

So they do the slow grind for the third time.

He gets out of bed when he's finished and she asks, 'Well I

suppose you're ringing up room service to get a bottle of champagne.'

He says, 'No, I'm ringing up Jack Nicklaus to find out the par for this hole!'

THE GOLF PRO

The golf pro walked over to two women and asked, 'Are you here to learn how to play golf?'

One replied, 'My friend is. I learned on Wednesday.'

Talk about fantastic golf teachers.

He was the best and one day this woman came to him and said that she had developed a terrific slice.

Day and night he worked with her for five months.

Now she's the biggest hooker in town.

Fred was playing off the sixth tee.

The fairway of the sixth needed some skill because it ran alongside the road.

But Fred sliced the ball badly and it disappeared over the hedge bordering the road.

So he put another ball down and took the penalty.

He was having a beer after the game when the pro joined him in the bar.

'Excuse me Fred, but was it you who sliced this ball into the road at the sixth this morning?' said the pro.

'Yes, but I took the penalty.'

'That's as may be. But you might be interested to know that your ball hit and killed a small boy on a tricycle; the tricycle fell in the path of a Mountie on a motorcycle. He skidded and was thrown through the window of a car, killing the nun at the wheel. The car then swerved into a cement mixer which wasn't too damaged but had to veer slightly and in doing so ran into the local school bus with such an impact that it sent it flying through the window of the shopping centre. At last count from the hospital there are 13 people dead and 79 people seriously injured.'

The golfer turned a deathly shade of white and said, 'What can I do?'

'Well, you could try moving your left hand a little bit further down the shaft,' the pro advised.

The tall Highlander walked into the pro shop at the Scottish golf club and stood ramrod straight as he carefully pulled a badly battered and nicked ball from his sporran.

'What can you do with this?' he asked the golf pro.

'Well,' said the manager in complete understanding, 'we can vulcanise it for five pence or re-cover it for ten.'

'I'll let ye know t'morra,' said the customer.

The next day he was back, holding out the ball.

'The committee met. Four votes to re-cover it,' he said, ' And three votes ta' vulcanise . . .'

'You surely don't want me to hole that?' the pompous amateur blustered.

His ball was about 30 cm from but his opponent, the club professional, answered quietly. 'No.'

The amateur picked up and walked onto the next tee.

He was about to take honour when he was interrupted by his opponent.

'My honour, I think,' said the professional. 'I won last hole, as you didn't putt out.'

'But you said you didn't want me to hole out,' spluttered the amateur.

'That's right. I didn't and you didn't.'

I don't know about that new pro,' said Peter. 'He may be a little strange.'

'Why do you think that?' asked Fred.

'He just tried to correct my stance again.'

'So?' said Fred. 'He's just trying to help your game.'

'Yeah, I know,' said Peter, 'But I was standing at the urinal at the time.'

When can you let me have another session?' a golfer asked his professional, who was a veteran of 75 years.

'Tomorrow morning,' came the reply, 'But not afternoon. That's when I visit my father.'

'Goodness me,' exclaimed the student incredulously, 'How old is he then?'

'Ninety-five.'

'And a good player too?'

'Ah, no sir—knocks the ball about a bit but, bless him, he'll never make a player.'

THE PRO'S PRAYER

The Pro is my Shepherd, I shall not Slice.
He maketh me to Drive Straight Down Green Fairways;
He leadeth me Safely across Still Water-Hazards;
He restoreth my Approach Shots.
He guideth me in the Paths of Accuracy for my Game's Sake.
Yea, though I chip through the Roughs in the shadows of Sand Traps, I will fear no Bogies.
For his Advice is with me; His Putter and Irons, they comfort me.

He prepareth my Strategy for me in the presence of mine Opponents; He anointeth my head with Confidence: The Cup will not be runneth over!

Surely Birdies and Eagles shall follow me all the Rounds of my Life;

And I will score in the Low Eighties,

Amen

The Justice of the Peace in a small town was about to tee off with two other friends one day when the club pro volunteered to join them.

It seemed like the perfect opportunity for a free lesson.

But instead of being helpful, the pro was openly critical of the JP's game.

At every bumbled shot, the pro made a joke about the good Justice.

The criticism didn't even stop at the end of the round.

The pro continued to embarrass the JP in the clubhouse among his friends.

Finally the pro got up to leave and said, 'Judge, let's do it again sometime. If you can't find anybody else to make a foursome, I'll be glad to play with you again.'

'Well that would be fine,' the Justice of the Peace said. 'How about next Saturday? I don't think any of my friends can join us, so why don't you just have your parents join us and after our round I can marry them . . .'

An amateur was talking to his golf pro.
Amateur: 'How do you get so much backspin?'
Pro: 'Before I answer that, tell me, how far do you hit a five iron?'
Amateur: 'About 130.'

Pro: 'Then why in the world would you want the ball to spin back?'

There were three men who wanted to learn how to play golf, so they hired a golf pro to help them out.

The pro asked the three men to hit the golf ball as far as they could.

One man hit way to the right. The pro yelled, 'LOFT!'

Then the second man hit it way to the left. The pro yelled, 'LOFT!'

Then the third man hit the golf ball two feet ahead of him. The pro yelled, 'LOFT!'

The three puzzled men asked the pro what 'LOFT' meant.

The pro simply said, 'Lack Of Friggin' Talent . . .'

The pro at the country club was rude.

When he beat you on the golf course he not only took your money he then told you everything you did wrong and suggested that you would never be able to hit the ball out of your own shadow.

One of the members had enough, so he bought a gorilla and trained it to play golf.

He then set up a game with the pro—$1000 a side with automatics.

The day of the match arrived and all parties were ready.

The first hole was a par five of 575 m.

The pro teed off splitting the fairway some 270 yards out.

The gorilla lumbered up to the tee.

He placed the ball on the ground and made a mighty swing.

The ball rocketed off the clubface 100, 200, 300, 400, 500, 575 m and stopped 5 cm from the cup.

The pro just about fell out of his pants.

If this was an indication of the way things were going to go, then he would never live it down.

He immediately settled the bet, remembering that he had urgent business across town.

As they walked from the tee the pro asked, 'How does he putt?'

'The same as he drives,' came the answer, '575 m . . .'

A retiree was given a set of golf clubs by his co-workers. Thinking he'd try the game, he asked the local pro for lessons, explaining that he knew nothing whatever of the game.

The pro showed him the stance and swing, then said, 'Just hit the ball toward the flag on the first green.'

The novice teed up and smacked the ball straight down the fairway and onto the green, where it stopped inches from the hole.

'Now what?' the fellow asked the speechless pro.

'Uh? Oh, you're, um, supposed to hit the ball into the cup,'
the pro finally said, after he was able to speak again.

'Oh great! So *now* you tell me,' said the beginner in a
disgusted tone.

A pro left his valuable golf clubs in the back seat of his car,
parked in a suburban shopping centre.

Concerned about them, he left a note reading, 'These prize
clubs belong to a fitness fanatic who is an ex-SAS soldier, a
heavyweight boxer and expert in karate and who will be back
in five minutes.'

When he came back, the clubs were gone and in their place
was a little note saying, 'Your clubs were taken by a Olympic
Marathon champion and I won't be back at all . . .'

B ill, the avid golfer, got married to Sally; but the marriage was
soon getting into problems as he was playing golf five days
a week.

They finally talked about it and Sally asked Bill if he could
teach her golf.

That way, suggested Sally, they both could enjoy golf and
improve their marriage. Bill argued that golf is a serious game
and that she was just trying to destroy the one perfect thing
in life.

After some heated discussion, Bill agreed to have her go to
the course with him.

They went to the course and Sally signed up to take some
lessons with the local pro. The lessons kept going on every day
and Bill was happy she didn't bother him.

One day, Bill's buddy Ralph asked him how the marriage was
going.

Bill replied, 'It is great; ever since she started taking golf lessons, she doesn't bother me and lets me play all the golf I want.'

Ralph replied with a sad shake of his head, 'Really? Then I guess you don't know that she is screwing around with the golf pro!'

Bill's eyes turned red, smoke came out of his ears and he became quite scary. He said, 'Damn! I knew it couldn't last; I knew Sally would make a mockery of the game!'

GOLF TRIPS

Did you hear about the women in the golf four that were staying at a country golf club?

They were told that although their quarters would be in a separate building, they were to mess with the men.

It wasn't until five days later someone finally told them that only meant to eat their meals with them . . .

Sherlock Holmes and Dr Watson were on a camping golf trip. They had gone to bed and were lying there looking up at the sky.

Holmes said, 'Watson, look up. What do you see?'

'Well, I see thousands of stars.'

'And what does that mean to you?'

'Well, I guess it means we will have another nice day tomorrow and the golf will be great. What does it mean to you, Holmes?'

'To me, it means some prick has stolen our tent.'

THE DRINK

Jock and an Englishman had just had a game of golf and were at the nineteenth hole when the waitress approached. 'May I get you something?' she asked.

'Aye, a whisky,' Jock replied.

She poured him a drink then asked the Englishman if he'd like one.

'Never!' he said sternly. 'I'd rather be raped and ravished by whores all the way to America than drink whisky!'

Jock hurriedly passed the drink back, saying 'Och, Ah didn't know there wuz a choice!'

An old golfer staggered home late after a day on the course and another evening with his drinking buddies.

Shoes in left hand to avoid waking his wife, he tiptoed as quietly as he could toward the stairs leading to their upstairs bedroom, but misjudged the bottom step in the darkened entryway.

As he caught himself by grabbing the banister, his body swung around and he landed heavily on his rump.

A whiskey bottle in each back pocket broke and made the landing especially painful.

Managing to suppress a yelp, he sprung up, pulled down his pants and examined his lacerated and bleeding cheeks in a mirror of a nearby darkened hallway, then managed to find a large full box of band-aids before proceeding to place a patch as best he could on each place he saw blood.

After hiding the now almost empty box, he managed to shuffle and stumble his way to bed.

Morning, he woke with screaming pain in head and butt to find his wife staring at him from across the room and heard her say, 'You were drunk again last night!'

Forcing himself to ignore his agony, he looked meekly at her and replied, 'Now, honey, why would you say such a mean thing?'

'Well,' she said, 'There is the front door left open, the glass at the bottom of the stairs, the drops of blood trailing through the house and your bloodshot eyes.

'But, mostly . . . it's all those band-aids stuck on the downstairs mirror!'

This man walks into the bar in a golf club with a monkey on his shoulders.

He takes a seat at the bar, lets the monkey go and orders a drink.

The monkey is running wild through the bar, swinging from the lights, jumping on the tables and showing off.

The monkey then jumps up on a display of golf mementos, grabs a golf ball and swallows it.

By now, the bartender is really annoyed.

The gentleman who owns the monkey apologises. He pays for his drink and the ball. Then he leaves with his monkey.

A couple of weeks later, the man returns with his monkey.

He sits at the bar and lets the monkey run wild again.

He jumps up on the bar where he spies a bowl of grapes.

He grabs a grape and shoves it up his ass, pulls it out and then eats it.

The bartender is totally grossed out.

'Did you see what your monkey just did?' he asks the man.

The man replies, 'Oh yeah, since that golf ball incident he measures everything!'

One day, after his weekly game of golf, Jock bought a flask of fine whisky from the club, put it in his pocket and while walking home he fell.

Getting up he felt something wet on his pants.

He looked up at the sky and said, 'Oh, Lord please, I beg you, let it be blood!'

A golf club barman, who was rather stingy with dishing out the whisky, was giving a member a drink.

As he handed the member his glass, the barman said it was extra good whisky, being 14 years old.

'Well, sir,' said the golfer regarding his glass sorrowfully, 'it's very small for its age . . .'

Sandy was drinking at the golf club all night.

When he got up to leave, he fell flat on his face.

He tried to stand again, but to no avail. He fell flat on his face again.

He decided to crawl outside and get some fresh air, to see whether that would sober him up.

Once outside, he stood up and, sure enough, fell flat on his face.

So, being practical, he crawled all the way home.

When he got to the door, he stood up yet again, but fell flat on his face.

He crawled through the door into his bedroom.

When he reached his bed, he tried once more to stand upright.

This time he managed to pull himself to his feet but fell into bed.

He was sound asleep as soon as his head hit the pillow.

He woke the next morning to his wife shaking him and

shouting, 'So, you've been out drinking as usual!'

'Why would you say that?' he complained innocently.

'Because the golf club called and you left your wheelchair there again!'

The golf club was concerned with the amount of binge drinking that was going on so they arranged for a temperance lecture to be given by Scotland's top medical man, a noted anti-drink campaigner.

The speaker began by placing a live, wriggling worm in a glass of whisky.

After a moment or two it died and sank to the bottom.

The speaker said quietly to the audience, 'Now my friends, what does this tell us?'

Jock piped up, 'If you drink whisky you'll not be bothered by worms!'

J ock was at a golf fund raiser and was seated next to a
stern-faced clergyman.

As Jock pulled out a bottle of whisky from his pocket the
clergyman glared and said reprovingly, 'Look here, I am 65 and
I have never tasted whisky in my life!'

'Dinna worry, Minister,' smiled Jock, pouring himself a dram.

'There's no risk of you starting now!'

GOLFING CLICHÉS

The captain of the club you wish to join turns out to be someone you were at school with and you never got on with.

The club secretary is always on the course when you want him, but is in the bar when your annual fees are overdue.

Whatever the rule for a particular situation, you've probably broken it.

The distant puff of sand you see means that your ball has not carried the bunker and what's more, it is plugged under the lip.

The fact that trees are 90 per cent air does not mean your ball avoided the remaining ten per cent of timber.

Waterproof trousers cannot be removed without falling over.

No successive swings are ever the same except when you hit consecutive shots out of bounds.

Nobody ever coughs on your follow through.

Out-of-bounds fences are located half a metre the wrong side of your ball.

When playing to a temporary green, your ball finishes stone dead to the hole cut in the proper green.

When there is one minute left to get to the first tee, a shoelace breaks.

When you are looking for your ball, it is found (a) when you have trudged back and put another ball in play, (b) when the five minutes search time has elapsed and (c) when you tread on it and incur a penalty.

When you can tear yourself away from the office for a rare midweek round you find yourself in the midst of a visiting society.

When you drive your car to a pro-am, you are caught in an impenetrable traffic jam.

Using an old ball for a shot over water does not mean you will avoid the splash.

The 'yips' is something that afflicts other people. Until now . . .

The waiting-list at the club you wish to join has just closed.

The love of your life either hates golf or is a better player than you.

The more you play a course the more obsessed you become with its dangers.

The newer the golf ball the more likely you are to lose it.

Your controlled draw rapidly develops into a chronic hook. Similarly, your controlled fade is, in reality, a vicious slice.

Your favourite golf sweater is the one that gets shrunk in the wash.

Your first hole-in-one is always achieved when playing alone.

Your greatest round takes place against an important business contact whom you can't afford to humiliate.

Your natural ability as a golfer is in inverse proportion to the amount of money you spend on new equipment.

If a good course is one where you play to your handicap or better and a bad course is one where you struggle to break 100, why are there so many bad courses?

If the club is burgled, your clubs are never stolen. And if they are, you are under-insured.

If there is one solitary tree located on a hole, your ball will find it with unerring accuracy.

If you are giving strokes in a match, it's always too many. If you are receiving them, it's never enough.

If you are playing well in a competition, your partner will tell you that if you keep it up you must win. This remark ensures that you finish with a string of double-bogeys.

If you find your ball in the woods, it is unplayable. If a professional finds his ball in the woods, not only is it playable but he can hit it onto the green.

If you score a hole-in-one during competition, you are in the last group and the bar is packed when you come in.

If you have difficulty meeting new people, try picking up someone else's golf ball.

Finding the key to a better game means opening a lot of doors.

Foursomes golf means always having to say you're sorry.

Golf is like sex. Afterwards you feel you should have scored a little better.

Golf is the only game in which you fail to win 99 per cent of the time.

Curly, downhill, left-to-right putts are usually followed by curly, uphill, right-to-left putts.

Delicate chip shots over bunkers always catch the top of the bank and fall back.

During the first round with a brand new set of clubs, the ball has to be played from a bitumen road.

Electric trolleys always break down at the furthest point from the clubhouse.

Always concede the fourth putt.

Bunkers have the unnerving habit of rushing out to meet your ball.

Coincidentally, the only remaining set of clubs in the professional's shop was made especially for you.

Curing the faults in your swing can never be effected in just one lesson from a professional.

A golf gift given to you at Christmas by a non-golfer is always unsuitable.

A vacuum is the space between your ears that becomes entirely void of matter once you set foot on the course.

After 36 holes in broiling heat, there are never any clean towels for a shower. And the bar has just closed.

All forms of wildlife on a golf course are there for the express purpose of putting you off.

Greens are hollow-tined and dressed the day before a competition.

Handicaps are designed to keep you in your place.

Hitting an iron off the tee for safety means same direction, less distance.

If a golfer wishes to give you a blow-by-blow account of his round, ask him to start with his final putt on the eighteenth green.

Shots that finish close to the pin are never as close when you get there.

Spike marks always deflect your ball away from the hole.

Teeing up on the side nearest the out-of-bounds means your ball will finish in the cabbage on the other side.

The ball nestling in a footprint in a bunker is invariably yours.

The reserve glove you have kept for wet weather has shrunk.

The sand in the bunkers is never the right texture for your particular technique.

The shorter the putt, the smaller the hole becomes.

The shortest distance between the ball and the target is never a straight line.

I SAY, I SAY

I got a putter for my wife.
Best trade I ever made . . .

Q: What do Tiger Woods and Billy Graham have in common?
A: They both can make 70,000 people stand up and yell, 'Jesus Christ.'

Two Irish golfers reach a very foggy par three.
It's the last hole of a tightly contested match, with a lot at stake.

They can just see the top of the flag—but not anything of the green.

Not to worry, their caddies say they will watch what happens when the balls land.

So, off the caddies go and both players take their shots.

When the players reach the green and look around, they find one ball a metre from the hole and the other in the hole.

The caddies ask what make and number ball the players were using, as they were unsure which one had holed out.

One player says, 'A Top-Flite, number 2.'

The other says, 'That's what I was playing, too!'

With that, everyone decides the only way to find a solution was to talk to the pro.

After hearing the story, examining the balls and congratulating them for their great shots, he asks the caddies, 'Okay, now which of them was using the orange ball . . .?'

Jesus, Moses and God were out playing golf one day. Jesus teed off first and the ball flew straight over the fairway, landed in the green and rolled to within a couple feet of the hole.

Moses hit second and his ball also soared and landed close to the hole.

Both looked over at God.

God took a few practice swings and then let loose on his ball.

The ball flew off into the rough.

Just then, a squirrel jumped over, grabbed the ball in his mouth and started running across the fairway.

An eagle swooped down and grabbed the squirrel in its claws, but before it could get too far, a bolt of lightning struck the bird.

The ball fell and a sudden gust of wind dropped it directly into the hole.

Jesus glared at God and said, 'Hey, are you here to play golf or just screw around?'

A young American golf fanatic, six months new to the game, decided to make the trip of a lifetime to Scotland, the holy land of golf.

Upon his arrival he quickly headed out to the course and arranged a tee time for a short time later.

As per his PGA teaching professional's instructions, he requested and secured the best caddie the course had to offer—Olde Angus, the pride of the links for 53 years.

Happily the young American set off on his dream round but 15 holes later numb and disgusted, 43 strokes over par, he reached over, grabbed his clubs and bag from Olde Angus and tossed them over the cliff into the churning sea below.

Turning to Angus and with the spittle of frustration coming

from his mouth he said, 'Angus, you are positively the worst caddie on the face of this earth,' to which Olde Angus replied, 'Nay, I dinna think that's possible laddie, it would be far too much of a coincidence . . .'

Greenkeeper Jock was digging away when a passing American tourist asks, 'How much land do you have here?'

'About 50 acres,' Jock replies.

'You know back home it takes me a day to drive around my ranch!' the American boasts.

'Aye,' says Jock, 'I once had a car like that.'

Q: What's the difference between a bad golfer and a bad skydiver?

A: A bad golfer goes, WHACK! 'Damn.'

A bad skydiver goes, 'Damn.' WHACK!

Have you heard about the lecherous Jock who lured a girl he had met at golf up to his attic to see his etchings?

He sold her four of them.

I had a great day at the golf today.

I found more balls than I lost . . .

'Do not trust him. He's a con man and, worse than that, he cheats at golf.'

'Oh, do you know him personally . . .?'

CARE AND ATTENTION

A Texan oil tycoon appeared at a local British golf course followed by a servant pulling a foam cushioned chaise lounge.

His outraged opponents thought that this was taking style too far and began to complain.

'Are you going to make that poor caddie lug that couch all over the course after you?' he was asked.

'Caddie, my eye,' explained the Texan, 'That's my psychiatrist.'

A couple of women were playing golf one sunny afternoon. The first of the twosome teed off and watched in horror as the ball headed directly toward a foursome of men playing the next hole.

Sure enough, the ball hit one of the guys and he immediately clasped his hands together at his crotch, fell to the ground and proceeded to roll around in agony.

The woman rushed over and immediately began to apologise.

She then explained that she was a physical therapist and offered to help ease his pain. 'No thanks, I'll be alright . . . I'll be fine in a few minutes,' he replied as he remained in the foetal position still clasping his hands together at his crotch.

But she persisted and he finally allowed her to help him.

She gently took his hands away and laid them to the side, loosened his pants and put her hands inside, beginning to massage him.

'Does that feel better?' she asked.

'Ohhh, Yeah . . . It feels really great', he replied, 'But my thumb still hurts like hell!'

Caddying for the elderly beginner had required great patience.

He was doddery but he was dogged and he had sworn to break 100 before the summer was out.

In fact there was a bottle of malt whisky riding on it—his faithful caddie would receive it when the magic score had been broken.

Then arrived a day when dogged persistence seemed about to pay off for both player and caddie.

They were on the green at the eighteenth and only 97 strokes had been accounted for.

Player and caddie were excited and in the grip of such emotion it was small wonder that the player sent his first putt racing 3 m past the hole.

In a flash the caddie had dropped the flagstick, picked up the ball and was crying excitedly. 'Well done, sir! You've done it! You've done it! Anyone would give you that!'

A man was playing golf one day.
He saw a snake with a frog in its mouth.

Feeling sorry for the frog, he reached down, gently took the frog from the snake and set the frog free.

But then he felt sorry for the snake.

He looked into his golf bag, but he had no food.

All he had was a bottle of bourbon.

So he opened the bottle and gave the snake a few shots.

The snake went off happy, the frog was happy and the man was happy to have performed such good deeds.

He thought everything was great until about ten minutes passed and he heard something in the grass at his feet.

With stunned disbelief, the golfer looked down and saw the snake was back with two frogs!

A male foursome was being held up by two rather slow lady golfers, one of whom was very frustrated, spending many minutes searching in the rough without any apparent success.

One of the blokes shouted to her partner, 'Why don't you help your friend look for her ball and we can get on with our game?'

'Oh,' came the reply. 'She's not looking for her ball. She's looking for her club . . .'

KIDS AND GOLF

A golfer came home from an extended hospital stay to find his eight-year-old son riding a new ten speed bike.

'Wow', he yelled, 'where did you get the money for that bike, son? It must have cost $500.'

'Dad, I earned it hiking,' said the boy.

'Hiking?' said the puzzled Dad.

'Yeah, every other night, while you were in the hospital, Mr Green from the pro shop came to see Ma.

'He'd give me $20 and tell me to go take a hike . . .'

A n eight-year-old boy and his six year-old brother were playing golf with their friends and practising both their game and their swearing.

The older boy suggested after the game that it was time they introduce their parents to their new talent.

He told his little brother, 'When we go back to the clubhouse I'll say "hell" and you say "ass".'

The six-year-old readily agreed.

As the two boys are seating themselves in the clubhouse for snacks their mother came in and asked how the game was.

The eight-year-old repied, 'Hell, Mom, it was good except I got a triple bogey.'

The surprised mother reacted with a swift whack on the boy's bottom and told him to go to the car.

The boy ran off crying and rubbing his backside.

With a sterner voice, the mother asked her younger son how his game was.

The boy replied, 'Okay, but you can sure bet your ass I didn't get a triple bogey . . .'

Johnny hates school and would much rather spend the day on the local golf course.

Consequently he often wags school and doesn't quite know what is going on there.

On one of the few occasions that he does turn up—it was too wet to have a hit—the teacher asked, 'Johnny, who signed the Declaration of Independence?'

He said, 'Damned if I know.'

She was a little put out by his swearing, so she told him to go home and to bring his father with him when he came back.

Next day, the father came with his son, sat in the back of the room to observe, as the teacher requested.

She started back in on her quiz and finally got back to the boy. 'Now, Johnny, I'll ask you again. Who signed the Declaration of Independence?'

'Well, hell, teacher,' Johnny said, 'I told you I didn't know.'

The father jumped up in the back, pointed a stern finger at his son and said, 'Johnny, if you signed that thing, you damn well better own up to it!'

LOCAL RULES

If a ball is swung at and missed

A player who assumes his stance, formally addresses the ball and then fairly strikes at it, but in so doing fails completely to make contact with any part of the ball, is deemed to have performed a full-address rehearsal of his swing (practice swing) and therefore need not count a stroke.

However, he must not show by either facial or verbal expression any disgust, frustration or provide any excuse.

Above all, he should not bag the course.

Ball renounced in flight

A player who hits a long, high drive that immediately travels in a clearly undesired direction may disown the ball while it is still in flight and instantly tee up and hit another without assessing a stroke for the first wayward shot.

Ball playable in water hazard, but just not worth it

If a player's ball comes to rest within the margins of a water hazard in a highly playable lie from which he is certain he could, if he so desired, hit a successful recovery shot with no difficulty whatsoever, but the marshy, muddy, swampy or boggy state of the surrounding terrain makes it inevitable that in the execution of such a stroke, he himself, his clothing or his equipment would be extensively soiled and/or soaked or that he would be obliged to assume a stance requiring the time-consuming removal of his footgear or other elaborate preparations, he may move his ball, without penalty, to the nearest equally favourable lie inside the hazard where conditions are sufficiently dry to permit prudent, sensible and reasonable play.

Ball not put fully into play
A player may replay any tee shot once, without assessing a stroke, if his ball fails to pass beyond the forward edge of the raised mound or grassy area comprising the ladies' tees.

Ball missing in fairway but obviously not lost
When a player cannot find a ball that he has clearly and unmistakably hit into the fairway, he may declare his ball to be 'missing but obviously not lost' and drop another ball in the approximate place where his original ball must have come to rest and play that second ball, without penalty of stroke.

Ball hit slightly out-of-bounds
If the ball lies just beyond the line of the out-of-bounds stakes and can be tapped, pulled, dragged or spooned back into bounds with any conforming golf club by a player standing within bounds and if the ball landed out-of-bounds but was clearly attempting to return within bounds when its progress was improperly blocked by mysterious forces beyond comprehension, then the ball may be dropped and played without penalty.

Ball hiding from player
If a player cannot find a ball that has been hit in plain sight into a reasonably playable area of the course where there is an accumulation of dead leaves, seasonal debris, grass clippings or other forms of incidental camouflage in which a furtive ball could improperly conceal itself, the ball shall be deemed to be hiding.

Audible interference with swing

A player may replay his shot without assessing a stroke if at any time during his backswing or downswing and prior to the moment when he strikes his ball, he shall hear a distracting sound or noise of any type, even though this sound may not have been heard by any of his playing partners and the source of it is unclear.

Agreement to re-tee

If all of the members of a playing group hit truly horrendous drives from the tee of the same hole, they may unanimously agree to replay their shots without assessing any strokes or incurring any penalties.

Administrative adjustment of scores

In order to allow for occasional imprecise recollections of strokes taken on a hole and to obviate the need for tedious recapitulations of play, any player who knows that he hit more than six shots on a hole but cannot say with certainty whether he hit a total of seven, eight, nine or ten shall return a score of seven on that hole.

Adjustment of lie prior to bold play

If a player declares his intention to hit his ball between, through, around or over any obstructing objects, he is entitled, by reason of his dauntless and venturesome play, to improve his lie, without penalty, by rolling or tapping his ball to a perfect lie.

ODE TO GOLF

In my hand I hold a ball,
white and dimpled, rather small.
Oh, how bland it does appear,
this harmless looking little sphere.

By its size, I could not guess,
the awesome strength it does possess.
But since I fell beneath its spell,
I've wandered through the fires of hell.

My life has not been
quite the same,
since I chose to play
this stupid game.
It rules my mind for
hours on end.
A fortune it has made
me spend.

It's made me swear and yell and cry.
I hate myself and want to die.
It promises a thing called par,
if I can hit it straight and far.

To master such a tiny ball,
should not be very hard at all.
But my desires the ball refuses
and does exactly as it chooses.

It hooks and slices, dribbles and dies
and disappears before my eyes.
Often it will take a whim
to hit a tree or take a swim.

With miles of grass on which to land,
it finds a tiny patch of sand.
Then has me offering up my soul,
if only it would find the hole.

It's made me whimper like a pup
and swear that I will give it up.
And take a drink to ease my sorrow,
but the ball well knows . . .
I'll be back tomorrow!

Anon

STAND-UP GOLF

He cut ten strokes off his score. He didn't play the last hole.

I'm not saying his game is bad, but if he grew tomatoes, they'd come up sliced.

I took a golf lesson yesterday and did really well. In just one lesson I was throwing my clubs as well as guys who have been playing for years!

I was under par after only four holes. A lovely bloke, Par!

A golf club is the kind of place where you meet the kind of people that you would have black-balled if you had gotten in before them . . .

It's a strange world isn't it? You hire someone to mow your lawn, so that you will have time to play golf for the exercise.

A Scotsman sadly gave up the game after 25 years. He lost his ball.

A mate of mine is known around the club as the James Bond of golf. After every hole, he says, 'Oh, oh, seven . . .'

B ad? I'll tell you how bad he is. In his bag he carries flares, a compass and emergency rations.

T he position of your hands is very important when playing golf.

I use mine to cover up my scorecard.

T he way he plays they should put the flags on the greens at half-mast.

H e had to get a new caddie on the ninth hole. He sent the first one back to the clubhouse for laughing too loudly.

T iger Woods is making so much money out of the game of golf, I hear he's got a drive-in wallet . . .

T he golf pro wants me to keep my head down so I can't see him laughing.

I played Tiger Woods once. There was only one in it. He scored 67 and I scored 167 . . .

There are thousands of people who are worse golfers than he is.
Of course, they don't play.

It seems to me that at times the hardest thing about golf is being allowed out of the house to play it.

He's too fat to play.
If he places the ball where he can hit it, he can't see it.
If he places it where he can see it, he can't hit it.

A doctor who golfs has one advantage over the rest of us.
Nobody can read his scorecard.

A mate of mine plays a fair game of golf.
But only when you watch him . . .

It seems to me that golf is just like life—you get yourself out of one hole and then you are in another.

I play with a golfer who is so accustomed to shaving his score that when he gets a hole-in-one he cards a zero.

Golf is an adult's way of playing marbles.

Nothing counts in a golf game like your opponent.

Is that my very dear friend stuck in the sand trap? Or is that the miserable bastard up on the green . . .?

John Daly is the only golfer who carries his own foursome.

Daly is so big that when he plays on the front nine, he casts a shadow over the back nine.

I am not the calmest golfer in the world. I once played nine holes and lost 11 clubs . . .

FOURSOMES AND PARTNERS

A foursome of senior golfers hit the course with waning enthusiasm for the sport. 'These hills are getting steeper as the years go by,' one complained.

'These fairways seem to be getting longer too,' said one of the others.

'The sand traps seem to be bigger than I remember them too,' said the third senior.

After hearing enough from his senior buddies, the oldest and the wisest of the four of them at 87 years old, piped up and said, 'Just be thankful we're still on the right side of the grass . . .'

Watching from the club house overlooking the tenth green, we saw a foursome approaching.

Having marked their balls, suddenly one of the guys fell down and the three others started a fist fight.

The golf captain stormed out from the club house to separate the men hurling punches at each other.

'Why are you fighting?' he asked.

'You see,' said one of them, 'My partner had a stroke and died just now and these buggers want to include it on the scorecard.'

Three friends play golf together every Saturday.

One day they were getting ready to tee off when a guy, by himself, asked them if he could join them.

The friends looked at each other and then looked at the man and said it was okay.

They teed off.

About two holes into the game, the friends got curious about what the lone man did for a living.

They asked him.

The stranger told them that he was a hit man, working freelance for a variety of gangsters.

The friends kind of laughed.

The man said, 'No, really, I am a hit man. My gun is in my golf bag. I carry it everywhere I go. You can take a look if you like.'

So one of the guys decided he would.

He opened up the bag and sure enough, there was this rifle with a huge scope on it.

He got all excited about it.

He said, 'Wow! I bet I can see my house through here! May I look?'

The stranger handed him the rifle.

The man looked for a second and said, 'Yeah! I can! I can even see through my windows into my bedroom. There's my wife, naked. Isn't she beautiful? Wait! There's my next door neighbour! He's in there. He's naked too!'

This upset the man.

He put down the gun, thought about it for a while, then he asked the hit man, 'How much would it be to, um, you know . . .'

The hit man replied, 'It's $1000 every time I pull the trigger.'

The man said, '$1000, ouch! Well, okay. I want two hits. I want you to shoot my wife right in the mouth. She is always nagging at me and I can't stand it. Second, I want you to shoot my neighbour right in the dick, just for screwing around with my wife.

'So, her mouth and his dick!'

The hit man agrees so he gears up and looks through the scope. He's looking for about five minutes.

The golfer starts to get impatient and asks the hit man what he is waiting for.

The hit man replies, 'Just hold on now . . . I'm about to save you a thousand bucks.'

A priest, a doctor and an engineer were waiting one morning for a particularly slow group of golfers.

Engineer: 'What's with these guys? We must have been waiting for 15 minutes!'

Doctor: 'I don't know, but I've never seen such ineptitude!'

Priest: 'Hey, here comes the greenkeeper. Let's have a word with him.'

George the greenkeeper comes over.

Priest: 'Say, George, what's with that group ahead of us? They're rather slow, aren't they?'

George: 'Oh, yes, that's a group of blind fire-fighters. They lost their sight saving our clubhouse from a fire last year, so we always let them play for free anytime.'

The group was silent for a moment.

Priest: 'That's so sad. I think I will say a special prayer for them tonight.'

Doctor: 'Good idea. And I'm going to contact my ophthalmologist buddy and see if there's anything he can do for them.'

Engineer: 'Why can't these guys play at night . . .?'

There's a foursome of ladies about to play a par three, 165 m long. Suddenly, out from the trees beside the fairway, a streaker runs across the open expanse of the fairway.

With a gasp, one lady remarks, 'I think I know that guy—isn't that Dick Green?'

'No,' replies another, 'I think it's a reflection of the grass!'

Once there was a beautiful woman whose two great joys in life were playing golf and working in her vegetable garden.

However, no matter what she did, she couldn't get her tomatoes to ripen.

She admired her golf partner's garden, which had beautiful bright red tomatoes.

One day while playing golf with him, she asked his secret.

'It's really quite simple,' the old man explained. 'Twice each day, in the morning and in the evening, I expose myself in front of the tomatoes and they turn red with embarrassment.'

Desperate for the perfect garden, she tried his advice and proceeded to expose herself to her plants twice daily.

Two weeks passed and her golf buddy stopped by to check her progress.

'So,' he asked, 'Any luck with your tomatoes?'

'No,' she replied excitedly, 'But you should see the size of my cucumbers!'

J ock decided to call his golf partner the 'Exorcist,' because every time he came to visit he made the spirits disappear.

A foursome of golfers was approaching the first tee when they noticed a woman being given first aid.

One of the golfers asked what had happened and he was informed that the woman had been stung by a bee and was having a reaction.

'Where was she bit?' he asked.

'Between the first and second hole,' came the reply.

He replied, 'Wow! She must have been standing right over the hive.'

F our guys who worked together always golfed as a group at 7 am Sunday.

But one of them got transferred and they were talking about trying to fill out the foursome.

A woman standing near the tee said, 'Hey, I like to golf, can I join the group?'

They were hesitant but said she could come once to try it.

She said, 'Good, I'll be there at 6.30.'

She showed up right at 6.30 and wound up setting a course record with a nine-under-par round.

The guys went nuts and everyone in the clubhouse congratulated her.

Meanwhile, she was fun and pleasant the entire round.

The guys happily invited her back the next week and she said, 'Sure, I'll be here at 6.30.'

Again, she showed up at exactly 6.30 Sunday morning.

Only this time, she played left-handed and matched her nine-under-par score of the previous week.

By now the guys were totally amazed and they asked her to join the group for keeps.

They had a beer after their round and one of the guys asked her, 'How do you know if you're going to golf right-handed or left-handed?'

She said, 'That's easy. Before I leave for the golf course, I pull the covers off my husband, who sleeps in the nude. If his member is pointing to the right, I golf right-handed; if it's pointed to the left, I golf left-handed.'

A guy asked, 'What if it's pointed straight up?'

She said, 'Then I'll be here at nine o'clock.'

Two women were put together as partners in the club tournament and met on the putting green for the first time.

After introductions, the first golfer asked, 'What's your handicap?'

'Oh, I'm a scratch golfer,' the other replied.

'Really!' exclaimed the first woman, suitably impressed that she was paired up with her.

'Yes, I write down all my good scores and scratch out the bad ones!'

A foursome of ladies came back after a round of golf. At the nineteenth hole in the clubhouse, the pro asked them, 'How did your game go?'

The first said she had a good round with 25 riders.

The second said she did okay with 16 riders.

The third said not too bad since she had ten riders.

The fourth was disappointed and said that she played badly with only two riders.

The pro was confounded by this term 'rider', but not wanting to show his ignorance just smiled and wished them better golf the next time.

He then approached Jerry the bartender and asked, 'Jerry, can you tell me what does this term "riders" mean?'

Jerry smiled and explained that a "rider" is when you have hit a shot long enough to take a ride on a golf cart . . .

The two golfers had been concerned for some time at the snail-like progress of a pairing of women originally some holes ahead and now just in front of them on the ninth fairway.

'I'll go up and ask if we can go through,' said Max to Jerry.

After walking about 50 m towards the ladies, Max suddenly turned around and scurried back to his playing partner.

'Jerry, this is very embarrassing, but would you mind going up to them? When I got closer, I realised that that's my wife up there and she's playing with my mistress!'

Jerry takes off, but quickly returns, having got no further forward than Max.

'Gee, Max,' he said, 'It's a small world . . .'

QUOTABLE QUOTES

As you walk down the fairway of life you must smell the roses, for you only get to play one round.
  Ben Hogan

If I had my way, any man guilty of golf would be ineligible for any office of trust in the United States.
  H.L. Mencken

When I'm on a golf course and it starts to rain and lightning, I hold up my one iron, 'cause I know even God can't hit a one iron.
  Lee Trevino

Golf is a game in which you yell 'fore', shoot six and write down five.
  Paul Harvey

Golf is a game where guts and blind devotion will always net you absolutely nothing but an ulcer.
  Tommy Bolt

Competitive golf is played mainly on a five-and-a-half inch course, the space between your ears.
Bobby Jones

I play with friends, but we don't play friendly games.
Ben Hogan

I'm hitting the woods just great, but I'm having a terrible time getting out of them.
Harry Tofcano

Golf is a good walk spoiled.
Mark Twain

Relax? How can anybody relax and play golf? You have to grip the club don't you?
Ben Hogan

The harder you work, the luckier you get.
Gary Player

The only shots you can be dead sure of are those you've had already.
Byron Nelson

The fun you get from golf is in direct ratio to the effort you don't put into it.
Bob Allen

Golf is 20 per cent mechanics and technique. The other 80 per cent is philosophy, humour, tragedy, romance, melodrama, companionship, camaraderie, cussedness and conversation.
Grantland Rice

Golf is a game whose aim is to hit a very small ball into an even smaller hole, with weapons singularly ill-designed for the purpose.
Winston Churchill

The players themselves can be classified into two groups: the attractions and the entry fees.
Jimmy Demaret

Let's see, I think right now I'm third in the money-winning and first in money-spending.
Tony Lema

There are no points for style when it comes to putting. It's getting the ball in the cup that counts.
Brian Swarbrick

You've just got one problem. You stand too close to the ball after you've hit it.
Sam Snead

Golf is based on honesty, where else would you admit to a seven on a par three?
Jimmy Demaret

The number one thing about trouble is . . . don't get into more.
Dave Stockton

Mulligan: invented by an Irishman who wanted to hit one more 20 yard grounder.
Jim Bishop

No one who ever had lessons would have a swing like mine.
Lee Trevino

Golf is 90 per cent inspiration and ten per cent perspiration.
Johnny Miller

Golf is an ideal diversion, but a ruinous disease.
Bertie Charles Forbes

Most golfers prepare for disaster. A good golfer prepares for success.
Bob Toski

A lot of guys who have never choked, have never been in the position to do so.
Tom Watson

I'm going to win so much money this year, my caddie will make the top 20 money-winners list.
Lee Trevino

Never bet with anyone you meet on the first tee who has a deep suntan, a one iron in his bag and squinty eyes.
Dave Marr

If you want to beat someone out on the golf course, just get him mad.
Dave Williams

If you try to fight the course, it will beat you.
Lou Graham

Putts get real difficult the day they hand out the money.
Lee Trevino

It's nice to have the opportunity to play for so much money, but it's nicer to win it.
Patty Sheehan

If you travel first class, you think first class and you are more likely to play first class.
Ray Floyd

It's the most fun I've ever had with my clothes on.
Lee Trevino

My best score ever was 103, but I've only been playing 15 years.
Alex Karris

Lay off for three weeks and then quit for good.
Sam Snead

Golf is the hardest game in the world to play and the easiest to cheat at.
Dave Hill

I've made a million, but I don't have a million.
Walt Zambriski

You don't know what pressure is until you've played for five dollars a hole with only two in your pocket.
Lee Trevino

Dams and lakes are sacrificial waters where you make a steady gift of your pride and high-priced balls.
Tommy Bolt.

Victory is everything. You can spend the money, but you can never spend the memories.
Ken Venturi

If you want to take long walks, take long walks. If you want to hit things with a stick, hit things with a stick. But there's no excuse for combining the two and putting the results on TV. Golf is not so much a sport as an insult to lawns.

National Lampoon

Golf is a fine relief from the tensions of office, but we are a little tired of holding the bag.

Adlai Stevenson

If you think it's hard to meet new people, try picking up the wrong golf ball.

Jack Lemmon

If you watch a game, it's fun. If you play it, it's recreation. If you work at it, it's golf.

Bob Hope

Give me my golf clubs, the fresh air and a beautiful girl for a partner. And you can keep my golf clubs and the fresh air!

Jack Benny.

RULES FOR BEDROOM GOLF

- Course owners reserve the right to restrict club length to avoid damage to the hole.
- The object of the game is to take as many strokes as necessary until the course owner is satisfied that play is complete. Failure to do so may result in being denied permission to play the course again.
- For most effective play, the club should have a firm shaft. Course owners are permitted to check shaft stiffness before play begins.
- It is considered bad form to begin playing the hole immediately upon arrival at the course. The experienced player will normally take time to admire the entire course with special attention to well formed bunkers.
- It is considered outstanding performance, time permitting, to play the same hole several times in one match.
- Play on a course must be approved by the owner of the hole.
- Players are advised to obtain the course owner's permission before attempting to play the back nine.
- Players are cautioned not to mention other courses they have played or are currently playing, to the owner of the course being played. Upset course owners have been known to damage player's equipment for this reason.
- Players are encouraged to bring proper rain gear for their own protection.
- Players should ensure themselves that their match has been

properly scheduled, particularly when a new course is being played for the first time. Previous players have been known to become irate if they discover someone else playing on what they considered to be a private course.

- Players should not assume a course is in shape for play at all times. Some players may be embarrassed if they find the course to be temporarily under repair. Players are advised to be extremely tactful in this situation. More advanced players will find alternative means of play.

- Each player shall furnish his own equipment for play—normally one club and two balls.

- Slow play is encouraged. However, players should be prepared to proceed at a quicker pace, at least temporarily, at the course owner's request.

- The course owner is responsible for manicuring and pruning any bush around the hole to allow for improved viewing of, alignment with and approach to the hole.

- Unlike outdoor golf, the object is to get the club in the hole and keep the balls out.

SMART ARSES

Two partners are ambling down the fairway, trying to outdo each other with stories of their golfing prowess.

'Well,' says the first, 'I once mishit a ball and it must have gone nearly 200 m, broke a window, hit an oil lamp, knocked it over and set the place on fire.'

The other bloke thinks about that for a while.

'So, then what did you do?'

'Well, I very carefully teed up another ball, steadied myself, took out the driver and belted the ball as hard as I could.

'It zinged through the air, onto the main road, shot past the bus stop, by the telephone booth and hit the fire alarm.

'Within two minutes, the brigade was on the scene putting out the fire.'

On the seventeenth hole, a very careful player was studying the green.

First he got down on his hands and knees to check out the turf between his ball and the hole.

Then he flicked several pieces of grass out of the way and, getting up, held up a wet finger to try out the direction of the wind.

Then turning to his caddie he asked, 'Was the green mowed this morning?'

'Yes, sir.'

'Right to left or left to right?'

'Right to left, sir.'

The golfer putted . . . and missed the hole completely.

He whirled on the caddie, 'What TIME . . .?'

Ah, easy! One long drive and a putt,' said the cocky golfer as he teed his ball and looked down the fairway to the green.

He swung mightily and topped the ball, which dribbled forward and landed about a metre in front of him.

His caddie slowly handed him a club and dryly remarked, 'And now for one hell of a putt . . .'

Real golfers have two handicaps: one for bragging and one for betting.

A pretty terrible golfer was playing a round of golf for which he had hired a caddie. The round proved to be somewhat tortuous for the caddie to watch and he was getting a bit exasperated by the poor play of his employer.

At one point the ball lay about 180 m from the green and as the golfer sized up his situation, he asked his caddie, 'Do you think I can get there with a five iron?'

And the caddie replied, 'Eventually.'

SOME AMAZING GOLFING FACTS

- The biggest number for one hole ever posted in a professional event is a 23 by Tommy Armour in the 1927 Shawnee Open. The previous week Armour won the American Open Championship.
- In 1995, a local member at a Lancashire Club sadly passed away. He was famous throughout the region as a wonderful straight hitter and won more club tournaments than anyone else in its history. His dying wish was for his ashes to be scattered on his beloved first fairway and his fellow members planned to honour this wish. However, as the ashes were scattered on the day of the ceremony, a gust of wind blew them out of bounds where they came to rest in a raspberry bush—the only time he had ever visited the spot!
- Legendary professional Harry Vardon, the greatest Open Champion of all-time, had only one hole-in-one during his long career.
- The 1978 PGA Colgate Championship had the largest field for a European Tour event with 398 players teeing up.
- Seven years later, in 1985, all European professional events were limited to 144 players.
- Mark Calcavecchia and John Daly were both fined by the US Tour for playing too quickly. They completed the final round in the Tournament Players' Championship in two hours and three minutes. Daly fired an 80 and Calcavecchia an 81.
- In the final round of the 1987 Open Championship at

Muirfield, Nick Faldo took a par on every hole to take the title.

- In the 1932 Walker Cup, legendary Cambridge Blue Leonard Crawley hit a wayward shot into the eighteenth green which resulted in hitting the actual Walker Cup trophy, putting a dent into it.
- In 1934 at St Margaret's-at-Cliffe Golf Club, Kent, WJ Robinson, the club professional, hit a drive on the eighteenth hole which resulted in hitting a cow in the back of the head. When Robinson and his playing partners reached the heifer, she was dead.
- New Zealand inventor Burton Silver has designed an oval golf ball. And he is serious. The new ball is based on the ball of the sport that the Kiwis love so much—rugby union. Silver claims he has spent 12 years developing the concept of his football-shaped golf ball and it is no spoof. In a new book called *New Zealand GolfCross*, Silver argues that the flight path of his oval ball is more predictable than that of the traditional round ball. 'The oval golf ball which, due to its two axis of spin, is more aerodynamically stable than the round ball,' according to his Web site. 'It's impossible to slice or hook, which is a huge advantage', he says.

STING IN THE TAIL

Once there was a golfer named Odd.
He was the butt of jokes his whole life, because of his name.

Eventually he grew up to be a very successful golfer, winner of several tournaments and owner of a country club.

When Odd was about to die, he said, 'People have been teasing me my whole life and I don't want them doing that after I'm dead, so don't put my name on my gravestone.'

But after Odd died, people saw his blank tombstone and would say, 'That's odd.'

A golfer stumbles into the nineteenth, approaches the only customer there and says, 'Hi, my name is Peter, could I buy you a drink?'

'Why of course,' came the reply, 'And my name is Paul.'

The introductions over, the question arose as to where Peter was from.

He said, 'I'm from Bainbridge, Georgia. I went to Bainbridge High and graduated in 1962.'

Paul was stunned for a moment, but said, 'I don't believe this. I went to Bainbridge High and I graduated in 1962.'

At this time, another customer came into the bar, sat down and asked the bartender, 'What's up?'

The bartender shook his head and said, 'Not much. The Brown twins are drunk again.'

A professor stood before his philosophy class and had some items in front of him.

When the class began, wordlessly, he picked up a very large and empty mayonnaise jar and proceeded to fill it with golf balls.

He then asked the students if the jar was full.

They agreed that it was.

So the professor then picked up a box of pebbles and poured them into the jar.

He shook the jar lightly.

The pebbles rolled into the open areas between the golf balls.

He then asked the students again if the jar was full.

They agreed it was.

The professor next picked up a box of sand and poured it into the jar.

Of course, the sand filled up everything else.

He asked once more if the jar was full.

The students responded with a unanimous, 'Yes.'

The professor then produced two cans of beer from under the table and poured the entire contents into the jar, effectively filling the empty space between the sand.

The students laughed.

'Now,' said the professor, as the laughter subsided, 'I want you to recognise that this jar represents your life. The golf balls are the important things, your family, your children, your health, your friends, your passions, things that if everything else was lost and only they remained, your life would still be full. The pebbles are the other things that matter like your job, your house, your car. The sand is everything else, the small stuff. If you put the sand into the jar first,' he continued, 'There is no room for the pebbles or the golf balls. The same goes for life. If you spend all your time and energy on the small stuff, you will never have room for the things that are important to you. Pay attention to the things that are critical to your happiness. Play with your children. Take time to get medical checkups. Take your partner out to dinner. Play another 18. There will always be time to clean the house and mow the lawn. Take care of the golf balls first, the things that really matter. Set your priorities. The rest is just sand.'

One of the students raised her hand and inquired what the beer represented.

The professor smiled. 'I'm glad you asked. It just goes to show you that no matter how full your life may seem, there's always room for a couple of beers.'

Ben, a top amateur golfer, went into the club bar and ordered six double vodkas.

Bob, the bartender said, 'Wow, you must have had a bad day.'

'Yeah', said Ben, 'I just found out my older brother is gay.'

The next day Ben showed up and again ordered six doubles.

Bob asked, 'What, more problems?'

And Ben replied, 'Damn right, I just found out that my younger brother is gay.'

The third day, the same routine—six doubles.

Bob said, 'What the hell! Doesn't anyone in your family like women?'

'Yeah,' said Ben, 'I just found out my wife does . . .'

A t 3 am, the manager of the local golf club receives a phone call at home from a man who sounds quite drunk.

The man asks the manager, 'Shay, pal, what time does the club open?'

The manager said, 'Ten o'clock', and he hangs up.

An hour later the phone rings again and the same voice asks, 'C'mon pal, what time does the club open?'

Again, the manager says, 'Ten am', and hangs up.

At 6.30 the phone rings and the same voice asks, 'Wenja shay the club opens again?'

The manager, now quite peeved, yells, 'I told you before, it opens at noon. And if you don't sober up, you won't get in.'

The slurry, drunken voice then says, 'Ah don wanna get in, I wanna get out . . .'

T wo friends, Bob and Earl, were very keen golfers. Their entire adult lives, Bob and Earl played and discussed golf.

When they weren't playing or talking about it they were either in the golf club or out raising funds.

They played at least three times a week and often more.

They even agreed that whoever died first would try to come back and tell the other if there was golf in heaven.

One summer night, Bob passed away in his sleep after playing eighteen holes of his best golf earlier in the day and then attending a club function at night.

He died happy.

A few nights later, his buddy Earl awoke to the sound of Bob's voice from beyond.

'Bob, is that you?' Earl asked.

'Of course it's me,' Bob replied.

'This is unbelievable!' Earl exclaimed. 'So tell me, is there golf in heaven?'

'Well, I have some good news and some bad news for you. Which do you want to hear first?'

'Tell me the good news first.'

'Well, the good news is that yes there is golf in heaven, Earl.'

'Oh, that is wonderful! So what could possibly be the bad news?'

'You're teeing off next.'

STRANGE BEHAVIOUR

Bob, whose handicap was 24, arrived at the first tee with his regular partners.

He took his driver and nailed it straight down the fairway like he had never done before.

His playing partners looked on in amazement but said nothing.

On approaching his ball, Bob took out a short iron and knocked it on to the middle of the green and thence proceeded to calmly two putt for par.

Again, nothing was said other than, 'Well played, Bob.'

This sequence continued for the next five holes with Bob even par through six.

The seventh was a really long and difficult par four of some 420 m.

Again, Bob drilled one down the middle—an unprecedented distance of 250 m.

By this stage, his playing partners' curiosity got the better of them and they asked him how he had done that.

Bob replied that he had just changed to new bi-focal glasses and when he looked down to address the ball he could see a big club and a little club, a big ball and a little ball so he hit the little ball with the big club—easy!

With 170 left to the green, Bob selected a seven iron and floated it right into the heart of the green.

Turning to his partners, Bob said, 'See, big club, little club, big ball, little ball—I hit the little ball with the big club—easy!'

When they reached the green, Bob lined up his putt.

It was a real animal—a 35 footer with double break over a

ridge to the hole tucked away at the back of the green.

Calmly, Bob stroked the putt and it sped into the cup without touching the sides. Birdie!

Stunned silence from his partners until one asked, 'How can you do that on your handicap?'

Bob's response was swift, 'I told you—these new glasses are great, I saw a big ball and a little ball, looked up along the line and saw a big hole and a little hole, so I hit the little ball into the big hole.'

On the next hole, Bob disappeared from the group for a few moments.

On his return, one of his partners observed that the front of Bob's slacks were all wet.

He inquired, 'What happened Bob?'

Bob replied, 'I went into the bush for a quick leak and when I looked down I saw a big one and a little one.

'I knew the big one wasn't mine, so I put it away . . .'

A n elderly lady from a remote little town went to one of Philadelphia's most fashionable suburbs to visit her niece and husband. Nearby was a very well known golf course.

On the second afternoon of her visit, the elderly lady went for a stroll.

Upon her return, the young niece politely asked, 'Well, Auntie, did you enjoy yourself?'

'Oh, yes, indeed,' said Auntie, beaming.

'Before I had walked very far,' she continued, 'I came to some beautiful rolling fields. There seemed to be a number of people about, mostly men.

'Some of them kept shouting at me in a very eccentric manner, but I took no notice. There were four men who followed me for some time, uttering curious excited barking sounds.

'Naturally, I ignored them, too. Oh, by the way,' she added, as she held out her hands, 'I found a number of these curious little round white balls, so I picked them all up and brought them home hoping you could explain what they're for.'

Two men were out playing a game of golf.

One of them was teeing off at the third hole, when a beautiful naked lady ran past. Naturally this distracted him somewhat, but the true committed golfer that he was, he resumed his stance.

As he was about to hit the shot again, two men in white coats ran past.

'What's going on here?' he thought, once again taking his stance.

Another distraction as a third man went running by in a white coat, but this man was carrying two buckets of sand.

Eventually, he was ready again and took his shot.

As he was walking down the fairway, he asked his companion what he thought had been going on.

His companion knew about all this and told him:

'Well once a week, that lady manages to escape from the mental hospital beside the course, tears off her clothes and runs across the fairways. The three guys you saw were the nurses. They have a race to see which can catch her first and the winner gets to carry her back.'

'What about the bucket of sand?'

'Well, that guy won last week, the buckets of sand are his handicap.'

SURPRISE, SURPRISE!

A minister, a priest and a rabbi were golfing on the hottest day of the year.

After 18 holes they were sweating and exhausted.

They decided to take a dip in the pool and to hide their clothes in the bushes so that nobody was aware that they were there.

They all stripped and jumped into the pond to cool down.

They were feeling refreshed and about to retrieve their clothes.

As they were crossing an open area in the nude, who should come along but the Ladies Auxiliary golf team.

The trio were absolutely shocked.

They decide to take quick action.

As they were caught unawares and unable to get to their clothes in time, the minister and the priest cover their privates.

And the rabbi covers his face.

After the ladies had left and they got their clothes back on, the minister and the priest asked the rabbi why he covered his face rather than his privates.

The rabbi replied, 'I don't know about you, but my congregation would recognise my face . . .'

A man was practising his putting at the local park when a genie appeared to him and told him that he could have one wish.

The man thought for a while and finally said, 'I have always wanted to go to Scotland to play the great golf course of

St Andrews, but I've never been able to go because I cannot fly. Airplanes are much too frightening for me. On a boat, I see all that water and I become very claustrophobic. So I wish for a road to be built from here to Great Britain.'

The genie thought for a few minutes and finally said, 'No, I don't think I can do that. Just think of all the work involved. Consider all the piling needed to hold up a highway and how deep they would have to go to reach the bottom of the ocean. Imagine the amount of pavement needed. No, that really is just too much to ask.'

The man thought for a few minutes and then told the genie, 'There is one other thing I have always wanted. I would like to be able to understand women. What makes them laugh and cry, why are they temperamental, why are they so difficult to get along with, when they want attention, when they don't. Basically, I want to be able to predict how they are going to react.'

The genie thought for a while and said, 'So, do you want two lanes or four?'

A man walked into the clubhouse and noticed a friend sitting in a corner wearing a neck brace.

He sat down and asked his mate what happened.

'Well, I was playing golf and I hit my ball into the rough,' replied his friend.

'Then I met a lady who was looking for her ball too. Finding mine, I thought I'd give her a hand. There was a sheep nearby and I noticed that every time it twitched its little tail there was a flash of white. So I went over to it and lifted its tail and sure enough there was the ball. I called out to the lady, "Ma'am, does this look like yours?" And the bitch hit me in the neck with her driver!'

Judge: 'Do you understand the nature of an oath?'

Boy: 'Do I? I'm your caddie, remember!'

The old Indian chief sat, smoking his ceremonial pipe, in his home on the reservation.

Nearby was a golf course, which wanted to add another 18 holes, which would be very close to the reservation.

Two officials were sent to interview him and see what he thought of the plan.

'Chief Two Eagles,' one official began, 'You have observed the white man for many years. You have seen all his progress and all his problems.'

The chief nodded.

The official continued, 'What do you think of all the white man has done?'

The chief stared at the officials for more than a minute and then calmly replied. 'When white man found the land, Indians were running it. No taxes. No debt. Plenty buffalo, plenty beaver. Women did most of the work. Medicine man free. Indian men hunted and fished and played all the time.'

The chief paused, then added, 'Only white man dumb enough to think he could improve system like that.'

A drunken golfer was seen crawling down some railroad tracks.

Asked if there was a problem, he replied, 'Yeah, can you help me off this ladder?'

Susan, the barmaid at the local golf club, was not the brightest of people, but an excellent drinks 'mixologist' — she could make any drink without referring to the bar manual.

One day, she ran in and yelled to the club pro, 'Fred, I just saw someone drive off in your new car.'

'Oh shit!' said the pro. 'Did you try to stop him?'

'No', she said, 'I did better than that. I got the licence number.'

THE BLONDE GOLFER

A blonde golfer goes into the pro shop and looks around, puzzled and frowning.

Finally the pro asks her what she wants.

'I can't find any green golf balls,' the blonde golfer replies.

The pro looks all over the shop and through all the catalogues and finally calls the manufacturers and determines that sure enough, there are no green golf balls.

As the blonde golfer walks out the door in disgust, the pro asks her, 'Before you go, could you tell me why you want green golf balls?'

'Well obviously, because they would be so much easier to find in the sand traps!'

This beautiful, very well endowed and shapely young blonde arrives at her course alone and joins a threesome of men.

Things go well for her. Getting through the round, with the help of tips and advice from the three men, she arrives at the eighteenth hole lying 98 with a two metre putt left to break the magic 100.

She tells the men, 'I have never broken 100 since I started playing golf two years ago and I am so anxious to break 100. If one of you men gives me the best tip as to how to sink this putt, I will reward him by making love to him right here on the green. He will enjoy the experience so much that he will remember it and tell all his friends the ecstasy he experienced for the rest of his life.'

The first guy checks the line and break from all sides and

suggests she just stroke it hard enough to drop it in the hole.

The second guy agrees, but tells her to hit it firm and slam dunk it in the hole.

She looks around for the third guy and finds him frantically undressing right down to his birthday suit.

She asks him, 'What on earth are you doing?'

'I'm getting ready for the love-making session,' he replies, tearing the last of his clothes off.

'But you haven't even given me your tip,' she says.

To which he replies, 'My advice is, pick the ball up. It's a gimmee . . .'

Two blondes are teeing off on a dull day on a par three—the last hole—as the evening is drawing in.

They can see the flag, but not the green.

The first blonde hits her ball into the dusk and the second golfer does the same.

They proceed to the green to find their balls.

One ball is about 2 m from the cup while the other has found its way into the cup for a hole-in-one.

'What ball are you playing?' says one blonde.

'A Hot Dot three,' comes the reply.

'Why, so am I,' says the other. 'How are we going to tell which is which?'

Just then, the pro, observing all this from the nearby pro shop, comes out and the blondes appraise him of their dilemma.

He looks at the ball on the green and the one in the hole.

'They are both great shots, girls,' he says.

'Now, which one of you is playing the pink one . . .?'

Two drunken blonde blokes were staggering home from the golf club up a dark country road.

'Hell, Mike,' says one, 'We've stumbled into the graveyard and here's a stone of a man who lived to 103.'

'I'll be darned, Joe. Was it anyone we knew at all?'

'No, it's someone named Miles, from Melbourne.'

THE GAME PLAYED IN HEAVEN

Two friends, Bob and Earl, were two very keen golfers. Their entire adult lives, Bob and Earl played and discussed golf. When they weren't playing or talking about it they were either in the golf club or out raising funds.

They played at least three times a week and often more.

They even agreed that whoever died first would try to come back and tell the other if there was golf in heaven.

One summer night, Bob passed away in his sleep after playing eighteen holes of his best golf earlier in the day and then attending a club function at night.

He died happy.

A few nights later, his buddy Earl awoke to the sound of Bob's voice from beyond.

'Bob, is that you?' Earl asked.

'Of course it's me,' Bob replied.

'This is unbelievable!' Earl exclaimed. 'So tell me, is there golf in heaven?'

'Well, I have some good news and some bad news for you. Which do you want to hear first?'

'Tell me the good news first.'

'Well, the good news is that yes there is golf in heaven, Earl.'

'Oh, that is wonderful! So what could possibly be the bad news?'

'You're teeing off next.'

An Irish priest loved to play golf.
It was an obsession of his.

So far this year the weather had been so bad that he hadn't been able to get out on the course at all, but as luck would have it, every Sunday the weather had been good.

However, on a Sunday he has to go to work.

The weather forecast was good again for the coming Sunday so he called a fellow priest claiming to have lost his voice and be in bed with the flu.

He asked him to take over his sermon.

The priest then drove fifty miles to a golf course so that no one would recognise him.

An angel up in Heaven was keeping watch and saw what the priest was doing.

He told God who agreed that he would do something about it.

The priest teed off and hit a wonderful shot. The approach shot was just as good and he putted brilliantly to get an eagle. This continued.

He was having the game of his life.

The priest chewed the course up achieving at least a birdie on each hole and sometimes an eagle.

In the end he broke the course record.

It was the game of his life.

Confused the angel asked God, 'Why did you let him have such a great golf game? I thought you were going to teach him a lesson.'

God replied 'I did. But who do you think he's going to tell . . .?'

Moses and Jesus were playing golf.
They came to a hole with a large water hazard in front of the tee box.

Moses took out his driver and Jesus took out his one iron.

Moses said, 'Hadn't you better use a driver?'

Jesus replied, 'No that's okay,' and took a swing which landed the ball in the middle of the water.

Moses parted the water and Jesus walked over and picked up his ball so he could drive it again.

Jesus kept his one iron, so Moses again asked, 'Shouldn't you use a driver?'

Jesus replied, 'No, that's okay,' and proceeded to drive the ball into the water once more.

Moses again parted the water so Jesus could retrieve his ball.

Jesus went back to the tee box and prepared to swing with the one iron again.

Moses finally said, 'Listen, if you hit that ball into the water again, I'm not going to help you get it.'

Jesus swung anyway and the ball went smack into the middle of the water again. Moses said, 'I told you I wasn't going to help you get that ball. If you want it, you will have to get it yourself.'

So, Jesus walked out onto the water to get his ball.

By this time the next group had caught up with them.

When they saw Jesus walking on the water, one of the golfers said, 'Who does that guy think he is? Jesus Christ?'

Moses replied, 'No, he is Jesus Christ. He just thinks he's Tiger Woods.'

A holy threesome went out to play golf in heaven. The first to tee off was Moses.

After teeing off, the ball went up the fairway and off into a pond.

So he walked up to the pond and as he started to step into the water, it parted.

He walked out to his ball and hit it up onto the green.

The next to tee off was Jesus.

He hit the ball up the fairway and it too went into the pond, only it stayed on top of the water.

He walked up to the pond and out on the water and hit the ball right up to the hole.

The next person got up and teed off.

It was a terrible hit.

The ball went off the fairway, went over and hit some guy's barn, bounced off the barn and rolled over into the edge of the woods.

In a few minutes a squirrel came along, picked up the ball and took it into the forest, went up a tree, out on a limb, and dropped it in a bird's nest.

The bird looked at the ball, then picked it up, flew out over the green and dropped it right in the hole.

Moses looked at Jesus, shook his head slowly and said, 'I hate playing golf with your father . . .!'

A husband and wife died and went to heaven together. They were met at the gates by an angel who was to show them the place.

'Right over here we have our very own golf course!' said the angel.

'Wow! It's beautiful! Can we play it now?' they both exclaimed.

'Sure,' said the angel.

So the couple began playing.

It was the most beautiful course they had ever seen.

Everything was perfect . . . the fairways, the greens, even the roughs.

The more they played the more the woman beamed with happiness, but she noticed her husband was becoming disheartened and angry.

The woman confronted her husband on what was wrong.

'I can't understand why you're not happy. We're in heaven! We're together! We're playing on the most beautiful and most perfect golf course ever! What's wrong with you?' she asked.

'If you hadn't fed us those damn bran muffins all that time, we'd have been here years ago . . .'

A man was golfing one day and was struck by lightning. He died and went to heaven.

St Peter told him when he arrived at the gates of heaven that the bolt of lightning was actually meant for his golf partner.

But, because God doesn't want it known that he makes mistakes, the man would have to go back to earth as someone other than himself.

Well, the man thought about it for awhile and announced to St Peter that he wanted to return to earth as a lesbian.

St Peter asked the man why a macho guy like him would choose to return as a lesbian.

The man answered, 'It's simple really, this way I can still make love to a woman and I can hit from the red tees!'

D ame Fortune was seldom kind to Sam.
Although Sam had a real zest for life he was constantly beset by bad luck.

He loved poker but poker did not love Sam; he played the stock market with great anticipation but always seemed to be the one who bought high and sold low.

His life seemed to be full of more downs than ups.

His greatest delight was his golf game.

Not that Sam was a great golfer; in fact, he never managed to break 100, but the odd shot that somehow ended up in the general area he had in mind was enough to keep his hopes alive.

Finally Sam became ill and passed away.

But just before he died, he asked that his remains be cremated and his ashes be scattered just off the fairway on the ninth hole of his home course.

Accordingly, a gathering assembled to carry out Sam's wishes.

It was a bright sunny day and was going well.

Then, as the ashes were being strewn, a gust of wind came up and blew Sam out of bounds . . .

H aving led an interestingly dissolute life composed largely of women, drinking, gambling and golf, but not necessarily in that order, at the end of it, the new arrival was not too surprised to find himself in Hell.

He was however quite surprised to find that his particular corner of Hades was an 18 hole golf course complete with gentle woods, a cool serene lake, well kept fairways, an immaculate green and a clubhouse with the usual professional's shop. The reprobate's delight was complete when he read the shop's notice, 'Help yourself—all equipment free.'

'Well, this is going to be tough to take,' he leered as he chose a bag containing perfectly matched clubs.

So laden, he ambled to the first tee where he took out a driver, gave a delighted practice swing and then felt in the ball pocket.

It was empty.

He was about to return to the shop to remedy the situation when he noticed a grinning figure in red.

'Don't mind me,' the grin grew wider, 'And don't bother going back for balls.'

'Why?' said the bewildered golfer.

'There aren't any. That's the hell of it!'

THE GOLF CLUB

He was a smooth operator and at the club's annual dance, he attached himself to the prettiest lady golfer in the room and was boasting to her.

'You know, they're all afraid to play me. What do you think my handicap is?'

'Well, where do you want me to start?' came the quick response.

A visiting golfer played 18 holes with his mates but needed to shower quickly and head back to his home town.

Having found the men's locker room showers full, his partners suggested he use the ladies showers as it was Saturday—members only day—so there would be no-one in there to bother him.

He had a great shower and just stepped out of the cubicle when three women walked into the locker room.

Quick as a flash he retreated into his shower cubicle.

One woman whispered to the other two, 'Is that a man in our shower?'

They replied that it was.

The woman asked her colleagues to kneel on the floor and look under the gap between the cubicle and the floor.

The first woman looked and could only see the man from the waist down and said, 'That's not my husband.'

The second woman repeated the exercise, looked and said, 'That's not my husband either.'

The third woman, a crusty old timer got down on her knees

and peered under the wall, stood up and proudly reported,
'He's not even a member at this club . . .'

A country club didn't allow women on the golf course.
Eventually, there was enough pressure that they decided to
allow women on the course during the week.

The ladies were satisfied with this arrangement, formed a
women's club and became active.

After about six months, the club board received a letter from
the women's club complaining about the men urinating on the
golf course.

Naturally, they just ignored the matter.

After another six months, they received another letter
reminding them of the previous letter and demanding action.

After due deliberation they sent the women a letter advising
them that they had been granted equal privileges!

The golf club maintenance man is a Scotsman.

One day, he and his offsider are instructed by the club manager to clean out an old septic tank near the ninth, to make way for a new bunker.

It's a warm day, so he takes off his jacket and drapes it over his shovel—where it slips off into the vast tank of poo!

He's just about to dive in when his mate shouts, 'It's nae guid tae do that, the jacket's ruined.'

He replies, 'Aye, but ma sandwiches are in the pocket.'

A man is struck by lightning while playing golf at an exclusive golf course.

He lies dying on the grass as a crowd of on-lookers gather around.

'A priest. Somebody get me a priest!' the man gasps.

The club captain checks the crowd—no priest, no minister, no man of God of any kind.

'A priest, please!' the dying man says again.

Then out of the crowd steps a little old man dressed shabbily and at least 80 years old.

The club captain agrees and brings the old-timer over to where the dying man lay.

He kneels down, leans over the injured man and says slowly in a solemn voice: 'Two little ducks—22; Ten—10; Two fat ladies—88; Lucky for some—13.'

When Jock moved to London he constantly annoyed his English acquaintances by boasting about how great Scotland was, what marvellous golf clubs they had and what great golfers he and his friends were.

Finally, in exasperation, one said, 'Well, if Scotland's so marvellous, how come you didn't stay there?'

'Well,' explained Jock 'They're all so clever up there I had to come down here to have any chance of making it at all.'

A golf club was located near a lunatic asylum and some of the more able patients spent a lot of time on the golf course and in the club rooms as part of their therapy.

However, they had to be granted a leave pass which was to be handed to the Course Manager, to say that they were okay, each time they came to the club.

A doctor of psychology was doing his morning rounds when he entered a patient's room.

He found his first patient sitting on the floor, pretending to saw a piece of wood in half.

Another patient was hanging from the ceiling, by his feet.

The doctor asked the patient on the floor what he was doing.

The patient replied, 'Can't you see! I'm sawing this piece of wood in half?'

The doctor then inquired as to why the other guy was hanging from the ceiling.

The guy on the floor says, 'Oh. He's my friend, but he's a little crazy. He thinks he's a light bulb Doc.'

The doctor looks up and notices the guy's face is going all red.

The doctor asks the wood cutter, 'If he's your friend, don't you think you should get him down from there before he hurts himself?'

And the patient replies—'What? And work in the dark!'

President Bush checked in at his exclusive golf club, ready to play a round with his minders, when he noticed a man in a long flowing white robe with a long flowing white beard and flowing white hair.

The man had a staff in one hand and some stone tablets under the other arm.

George approached the man and inquired, 'Aren't you Bin Laden?'

The man ignored George and stared at the ceiling.

George positioned himself more directly in the man's view and asked again, 'Are you Bin Laden?'

The man continued to peruse the ceiling.

George tugged at the man's sleeve and asked once again, 'Hey! Aren't you Bin Laden?'

The man finally responded in a very irate voice, 'No, I am not. I am Moses!'

George asked him why he was so uppity and had taken so long to answer him.

The man replied, 'Listen pal and listen good. The last time I spoke to a Bush, I ended up stuck in a desert for 40 years!'

Two gas company servicemen, a senior training supervisor and a young trainee, were out checking meters in a suburban golf club.

They parked their truck at the end of the alley and walked to the other end.

A woman who was sitting in the bar having a lemon, lime and bitters watched the two men as they checked the gas meter.

Finishing the meter check, the senior supervisor challenged his younger co-worker to a foot race down the alley back to the truck to prove that an older guy could outrun a younger one.

As they came running up to the truck, they realised the lady from the bar was huffing and puffing right behind them.

They stopped and asked her what was wrong.

Gasping for breath, she replied, 'When I see two gas men running as hard as you two were, I figured I'd better run too!'

THE SCOTTISH GOLF CLUB NOTICE BOARD

- Lost—a £5 note. Sentimental value.
- Increase the life of your carpets by rolling them up and keeping them in the garage.
- 'Lost, wallet containing £10,000. A reward of £100 to the person who finds it.'
  Underneath, written in pencil, 'I'll give £150!'
- Buy our Double Glazing so that the children cannot hear the ice-cream van when it comes round.

A woman is looking to re-enter the work force, now that her kids are all grown up. She is a successful applicant to become the Office Manager at the local golf club, but she needs to go to the doctor's to have a physical examination in order to obtain a certificate for the superannuation fund.

When she returns her hubby notices she's just busting with pride and all chuffed.

So he says, 'What's all this about?'

She says, 'I've just been tae the doctors' and he said I've got the body of a 20 year old and the heart of a 16 year old.'

To which her hubby fires back, 'What about your 50 year old ass?'

'Your name never came up,' she replies.

Angus called in to see his friend Donald to find he was stripping the wallpaper from the walls of the clubrooms.

Rather obviously, he remarked, 'You're decorating, I see,' to which Donald replied: 'No. We're moving into bigger rooms.'

The Mafia sponsors a local golf club as they find it is the ideal place to do business away from the prying eyes of the law.

Besides, many of the local businessmen that they do deals with frequent the club on a regular basis.

The Godfather was looking for a new man to make weekly collections from all the private businesses that they were 'protecting'.

Feeling the heat from the police force, they decided to use a deaf person for this job—if he were to get caught, he wouldn't be able to communicate to the police what he was doing.

On his first week, the deaf collector picks up over $50,000.

He gets greedy, decides to keep the money and stashes it in a safe place.

The Mafia soon realises that their collection is late and sends some of their hoods after the deaf collector.

The hoods find the deaf collector and ask him where the money is.

The deaf collector can't communicate with them, so the Mafia drags the guy to an interpreter.

The Mafia hood says to the interpreter, 'Ask him where da money is.'

The interpreter signs, 'Where's the money?'

The deaf collector replies, 'I don't know what you're talking about.'

The interpreter tells the hood, 'He says he doesn't know what you're talking about.'

The hood pulls out a .38 gun and places it in the ear of the deaf collector.

'Now ask him where da money is.'

The interpreter signs, 'Where is the money?'

The deaf man replies, 'The $50,000 is down on the seventeenth, hidden in the hollow tree near the sand trap on the left hand side of the green.'

The interpreter says to the hood, 'He says he still doesn't know what you're talking about and doesn't think you have the balls to pull the trigger.'

A Scotsman took a girl home from the Golf Club in a taxi. She was so beautiful he could hardly keep his eye on the meter.

An Australian golfer whose club had reciprocal rights went to a country course in the USA to play.

As he paid his bill, he asked the manager, 'By the way, what's with the Indian chief sitting in the lobby? He's been there ever since I arrived.'

'Oh that's "Big Chief Forget-Me-Not,"' said the manager. 'The club is built on an Indian reservation and part of the agreement is to allow the chief free use of the premises for the rest of his life. He's known as "Big Chief Forget-Me-Not" because of his phenomenal memory. He is 92 and can remember even the slightest detail of his life.'

As he was waiting for his cab, the golfer decided to put the chief's memory to the test. 'Hello, mate!' said the Aussie, receiving only a slight nod in return. 'What did you have for breakfast on your 21st birthday?'

'Eggs,' was the chief's instant reply, without even looking up and indeed the Aussie was impressed.

He went off on his travel itinerary, right across to the east coast and back, telling others of Big Chief Forget-Me-Not's great memory.

Returning to play at the club six months later, he was surprised to see Big Chief Forget-Me-Not still sitting in the lobby, large as life, fully occupied with whittling away on a stick.

Remembering that one local had informed him that 'How' was a more appropriate greeting for an Indian chief rather than 'Hello mate,' the Aussie greets him with, 'How?'

'Scrambled,' replied the Chief.

I n a small country town where the golf club is the gathering place for the locals, everyone knows each other.

During a court case, the prosecuting attorney called his first witness to the stand in a trial, a grandmotherly, elderly woman.

He approached her and asked, 'Mrs. Jones, do you know me?'

She responded, 'Why, yes, I do know you Mr. Williams. I know you from the golf club and I've known you since you were a young boy. And frankly, you've been a big disappointment to me. You lie, you cheat on your wife; you manipulate people and talk about them behind their backs. You think you're a rising big shot when you haven't the brains to realise you never will amount to anything more than a two-bit paper pusher. Yes, I know you.'

The lawyer was stunned. Not knowing what else to do he pointed across the room and asked, 'Mrs. Williams, do you know the defence attorney?'

She again replied, 'Why, yes I do. I've known Mr. Bradley since he was a youngster, too. He is a member at the golf club; I used to baby sit him for his parents. And he, too, has been a real disappointment to me. He's lazy, bigoted, he has a drinking problem. The man can't build a normal relationship with anyone and his law practice is one of the shoddiest in the entire state. Yes, I know him.'

At this point, the judge rapped the courtroom to silence and called both counsellors to the bench.

In a very quiet voice, he said with menace, 'If either of you asks her if she knows me, you'll be jailed for contempt!'

A Scots boy comes home from school and tells his mother he has been given a part in the school play.

'Wonderful,' says the mother, 'What part is it?'

The boy says, 'I play the part of the Scottish husband who plays golf.'

The mother scowls and says, 'Go back and tell your teacher you want a speaking part.'

TRICKY QUESTIONS

ACTUAL ANSWERS GIVEN AT A GOLF CLUB FUNDRAISING TRIVIA NIGHT

Name something a blind person might use	A sword
Name a song with moon in the title	Blue Suede Moon
Name a bird with a long neck	Naomi Campbell
Name an occupation where you need a torch	A burglar
Name a famous brother and sister	Bonnie and Clyde
Name an item of clothing worn by the 3 musketeers	A horse
Name something that floats in the bath	Water
Name something you wear on the beach	A deckchair
Name something Red	My cardigan
Name a famous cowboy	Buck Rogers
Name a famous royal	Mail
A number you have to memorise	Seven
Something you do before going to bed	Sleep
Something you put on walls	Roofs
Something in the garden that's green	Shed
Something that flies that doesn't have an engine	A bicycle with wings
Something you might be allergic to	Skiing
A famous bridge	The one over troubled waters
Something a cat does	Goes to the toilet
Something you do in the bathroom	Decorate
Name an animal you might see at the zoo	A dog
Something associated with the police	Pigs
A sign of the zodiac	April

Something slippery	A conman
A kind of ache	Fillet O' Fish
A food that can be brown or white	Potato
A jacket potato topping	Jam
A famous Scotsman	Jock
Another famous Scotsman	Vinnie Jones
Something with a hole in it	Window
A non living object with legs	Plant
A domestic animal	Leopard
A part of the body beginning with 'N'	Knee
A way of cooking fish	Cod
Something people have one of	Cricket bat
Something you open other than a door	Your bowels
Something you clean	Your sister

THE GOLF WIDOW

Mrs O'Brien came into the newsroom to pay for her husband's obituary.

She was told by the kindly newsman that it was a dollar a word and he remembered Pete and wasn't it too bad about him passing away.

She thanked him for his kind words and bemoaned the fact that she only had two dollars.

But she wrote out the obituary, 'Pete died.'

The newsman said he thought old Pete deserved more and he'd give her three more words at no charge.

Mrs Pete O'Brien thanked him and rewrote the obituary: 'Pete died. Clubs for sale.'

Fred called his friend in tears.

'I can't believe it,' he sobbed. 'My wife left me for my golfing partner.'

'Get a hold of yourself, man,' said his friend. 'There are plenty of other women out there.'

'Who's talking about her?' said Fred. 'He was the only guy that I could ever beat!'

'You're so involved with golf,' whined the wife, 'that you can't even remember the day we were married.'

'That's what you think!' countered the husband. 'It was the same day I sank a 35 foot putt.'

A wife begins to get a little worried because her husband has not arrived home on time from his regular Saturday afternoon golf game.

As the hours pass she becomes more and more concerned until, at 8 pm, the husband finally pulls into the driveway.

'What happened?' says the wife. 'You should have been home hours ago!'

'Harry had a heart attack at the third hole,' replied the husband.

'Oh, that's terrible,' says the wife. 'That must have ruined the whole day.'

'It sure did,' the husband answers. 'There I was for the rest of the round, hit the ball, drag Harry, hit the ball, drag Harry . . .'

A man playing as a single at an exclusive golf club was teamed with a twosome. After a few holes, the twosome finally asked why he was playing such a beautiful course by himself.

He replied that he and his wife had played the course every year—for over 20 years—but this year she had passed away and he kept the tee time in her memory.

The twosome commented that they thought certainly someone would have been willing to take her spot.

'So did I,' he said, 'But they all wanted to go to the funeral.'

A guy stood over his tee shot for what seemed an eternity; looking up, looking down, measuring the distance, figuring the wind direction and speed.

He was driving his partner nuts.

Finally his exasperated partner says, 'What's taking so long? Hit the blasted ball!'

The guy answers, 'My wife is up there watching me from the clubhouse. I want to make this a perfect shot.'

'Forget it, man! You don't stand a chance of hitting her from here!'

A golfer's wife asked him why he never would let her play golf with him.

'My dear,' he replied, 'There are three things a man must do alone: testify, die and putt . . .'

To Bill's wife, golf was a total mystery. She never could understand why he insisted on tiring himself by walking so far every time he played.

One day she went with him to see for herself what the game was about.

For six holes, she tramped after him.

It was on the seventh that he landed in the infamous bunker where he floundered about for some time in the sand.

She sat herself down composedly and, as the sand began to fly she happily ventured, 'There, I knew you could just as well play in one place if you made up your mind to!'

After the keen golfer comes home from a long round of golf, his wife kisses him and then kisses their son who comes in a few moments later.

'Where's he been?' the husband asks.

'He's been caddying for you all afternoon!' the astounded wife replies.

'No wonder he looks so familiar . . .!'

A guy gets a call from the coroner, who wants to talk about his wife's recent death.

'We were on the third hole,' the widower relates.

'My wife was standing on the ladies tee about 30 yards ahead of the men's, when I hit my drive.

'From the sound of it, when the ball hit her head and the way she dropped like a rock, I knew immediately that she was dead.

'God only knows where the ball wound up.'

The coroner replies, 'That explains the injury to her head, but what about the Maxfli ball embedded in her rectum?'

'Oh,' says the man, 'that was my provisional . . .'

'Darling,' asked the wife. 'What would you do if I died?'

'Why, dear, I would be extremely upset,' answered the husband. 'Why do you ask such a horrid question?'

'Would you remarry?' persevered the wife.

'No, of course not, love,' replied the husband.

'Do you like being married?' asked the wife.

'Of course I do, lamb,' he said.

'Then why wouldn't you remarry?'

'All right,' said the husband on taking a different tact trying to end the conversation, 'I'd remarry, then.'

'You would?' responded the wife, looking quite pained.

'Yes,' replied the trapped husband.

'Would you sleep with her in our bed?' asked the wife after a very long pause.

'Well, yes, I suppose I would,' replied her tiring mate.

'I see,' said the wife quite sternly and indignantly. 'And would you let her wear my old clothes?'

'I suppose, if she wanted to,' stammered her mate, adding, 'it would be a compliment to your exquisite taste.'

'Really,' replied the wife icily. 'And would you take down the pictures of me and replace them with pictures of her?'

'I don't know. But wouldn't that be the correct thing to do?,' he replied.

'Is that so?' said the wife, leaping to her feet. 'And I suppose you'd let her play with my golf clubs, too.'

'Of course not, dear. That would be impossible. She's left-handed . . .'

Q: How can a keen golfer tell if his wife is dead?
A: The sex is the same, but the dishes pile up.

You'll never hear a golfer's wife say, 'Shouldn't you be down at the bar with your friends?'

Happily innocent of all golfing lore, Sam's wife watched with interest the efforts of her man in the bunker to play his ball.

At last it rose amid a cloud of sand, hovered in the air and then dropped on the green and rolled into the hole.

'Oh my stars,' Sam's wife chuckled, 'He'll have a tough time getting out of that one . . .'

There was a guy so addicted to golf that all he did was go out on the links every single day.

He had ambitions of making it to the pros, so he took his game very seriously.

One windy day while playing in the finals of a tournament, the guy was in contention, so he played every shot with utmost care and concentration.

After all the scores were submitted, he was declared the winner of the tournament.

He went home to his wife with the trophy and some small cash prize.

He kept repeating his round over dinner.

The wife, who was not the least bit interested in golf, got up and went to bed early.

The guy followed after a few hours, still high on his golf championship.

At around two in the morning, the wife jumped up and screamed at her husband, who also gets startled and wakes up.

'What happened? Why are you screaming?' the guy asked his wife.

'Why wouldn't I shout? You just pulled a patch of hair from my privates and threw it up in the air!'

Four married guys go golfing.
Pretty soon they start talking about how difficult it is to get away from the wife and home to play.

First guy: 'You have no idea what I had to do to be able to come out golfing this weekend. I had to promise my wife that I will paint every room in the house next weekend.'

Second guy: 'That's nothing, I had to promise my wife that I will build her a new deck for the pool.'

Third guy: 'Man, you both have it easy! I had to promise my wife that I will remodel the kitchen for her.'

They continue to play when they realised that the fourth guy has not said a word.

So they ask him. 'You haven't said anything about what you had to do to be able to come golfing this weekend.'

'What's the deal?' says the fourth guy:

'I just set my alarm for 5.30 am. When it goes off, I burp, fart, scratch my balls, give the wife a nudge and say, "Golf course or intercourse".'

And she says, 'Don't forget your sweater . . .'

An elderly golfer was at home, dying in bed, when he smelled his favourite aroma—chocolate chip biscuits baking.

He wanted one last cookie before he died, so he crawled to the kitchen, reached up to the cookie sheet on the table and grasped a warm, moist biscuit.

His wife suddenly hit his hand with a spatula and yelled, 'Leave them alone. They're for the funeral.'

One day, two guys, Joe and Bob, were out playing golf. A funeral service passes by and Bob takes off his hat and puts it over his heart.

He does this until the funeral service passes by.

Joe then said, 'Gee Bob, I didn't know you had it in you!'

Bob then replies, 'It's the least I could do. After all I was married to her for 30 years.'

This guy and his wife were out golfing with another couple when he hit a 200 metre drive and ended up behind a barn just off the fairway.

He took out a wedge intending to go over to the barn when one of the guys suggested that they open both barn doors.

This they did and he takes a five iron, hits through the barn for a two putt par. So he tries it, hits the side of the barn and the ball comes back, hits his wife in the head and kills her.

About two years later, he finds himself in the same situation.

It is again suggested that he use a five iron through the open barn doors.

He shakes his head and says that he is not going to make the same mistake this time.

'Last time I tried that, the result was disastrous,' he said.

'I took a double bogey . . .'

Father O'Grady was saying his goodbyes to the parishioners after his Sunday morning service as he always does, when Mary Clancy came up to him in tears.

She was a golf widow whose husband spent every spare minute on the golf course.

'What's bothering you so, dear?' inquired Father O'Grady.

'Oh, father, I've got terrible news,' replied Mary.

'Well what is it, Mary?'

'Well, my husband, passed away last night, Father, straight after coming home from the golf club.'

'Oh, Mary,' said the father, 'that's terrible. Tell me Mary, did he have any last requests?'

'Well, yes he did father,' replied Mary.

'What did he ask, Mary?'

Mary replied, 'He said, "Please, Mary, put down the gun . . .".'

Anotorious golfer who always lied about his score had such a bad round he went home and when his wife said, 'How'd you go today, dear?' lost his head and beat the poor woman to death.

A little later, overcome with guilt, he rang the police and said, 'I've just killed my wife.'

He gave the police his name and address and about a minute later a police car screeched up the driveway and two policemen got out and banged on the door.

Police: 'Are you the man who said he killed his wife?'

Golfer: 'Yes, that was me.'

Police: 'Well, where's the body?'

The golfer took the policemen into the kitchen where a woman lay motionless on the floor. A policeman took out his pen and folder and started to take notes.

Police: 'Is this woman dead?'

Golfer: 'Yes.'

Police: 'And she is your wife?'

Golfer: 'Yes.'

Police: 'And you killed her?'

Golfer: 'Yes.'

Police: 'How did you kill her?'

Golfer: 'I beat her to death with my one iron.'

Police: 'How many times did you actually hit her?'

Golfer: 'Five—but put me down for four . . .'

A guy named Bob receives a free ticket to the Masters from his company. Unfortunately, when Bob arrives at the course, he realises that he hasn't got a seat, that he will have to stand all day.

About halfway through the day, Bob notices an empty seat in the gallery that surrounds the eighteenth hole. He decides to take a chance and makes his way to the empty seat.

As he sits down, he asks the gentleman sitting next to him, 'Excuse me, is anyone sitting here?' The man says no.

Now, very excited to be in such a great seat for the game, Bob again inquires of the man next to him, 'This is incredible! Who in their right mind would have a seat like this at the Masters and not use it?'

The man replies, 'Well, actually, the seat belongs to me, I was supposed to come with my wife, but she passed away. This is the first Masters that we haven't been to together since we got married in 1967.'

'Well, that's really sad,' says Bob, 'But still, couldn't you find someone to take the seat? A relative or a close friend?'

'Tried that,' the man replies, 'But they're all at the funeral.'

GOLFING IS BETTER THAN SEX BECAUSE:

- It's perfectly respectable to play golf with a total stranger.
- If you damage a ball it is easy to replace it with a new one.
- If your regular golfing partner isn't available, no one will object if you play golf with someone else.
- It is perfectly acceptable to pay a professional to play golf with you once in a while.
- If your partner takes pictures or videotapes of you playing golf, you don't have to worry about them showing up on the Internet if you become famous.

- The lay is always different.
- Nobody expects you to give up golfing if your partner loses interest in it.
- Nobody expects you to play golf with the same partner for the rest of your life.
- Nobody will ever tell you that you will go blind if you play golf by yourself.
- The ten commandments don't say anything about golfing.
- There are no golf-transmitted diseases.
- When dealing with a golfing pro, you never have to wonder if they are really an undercover cop.
- You can have a golfing calendar on your wall at the office, tell golfing jokes and invite co-workers to golf with you without getting sued for harassment. You don't have to go to a sleazy shop in a seedy neighbourhood to buy golfing gear.
- You don't have to hide your golfing magazines.
- Your golfing partner doesn't get upset about people you played golf with long ago.
- Your golfing partner will never say, 'Not again? We just played golf last week! Is golf all you ever think about?'
- A hole-in-one is applauded.

THOUGHTS TO PONDER

Real golfers don't miss putts, they get robbed.

Work is for those who don't play golf.

Play golf now. You are dead a long time.

I spent most of my life playing golf, the rest I wasted.

Playing golf is the second greatest thrill known to man. A hole-in-one is the first.

Noah played golf from his Ark because he only had two balls and he didn't want to lose one.

The difference between a fairy tale and a golf story? A fairy tale begins, 'Once upon a time . . .'
And a golf story begins, 'This ain't no bullshit . . .'

Man blames fate for other accidents that befall him, but takes full responsibility for a hole in one.

A caddie is now called 'a fairway technician'.

WISHFUL THINKING

Aman was playing a round on his local course one afternoon when a genie appeared to him and told him that he could have one wish.

The man thought for a while and finally said, 'I have always wanted to go to the States and play the great golf course Augusta where they play the Masters. But I've never been able to go because I'm an extremely bad traveller. I cannot fly because I get airsick and on a boat, I see all that water and I become sea sick. So I wish for a road to be built from here to Georgia.'

The genie thought for a few minutes and finally said, 'No, I don't think I can do that. Just think of all the work involved. Consider all the piling needed to hold up a highway and how deep they would have to go to reach the bottom of the ocean. Imagine the amount of pavement needed. No, that really is just too much to ask.'

The man thought for a few minutes and then told the genie, 'There is one other thing I have always wanted. I would like you to turn my wife into looking like Kylie Minogue. I love her very dearly, but she was behind the door when they gave out looks and time has not helped over the years. It would be great if you could make her look like Kylie.'

So the genie says, 'Do you have a picture.'

'As a matter of fact, I do,' says the golfer. 'I love her so much, I always keep one in my golf bag, just for luck.'

He rattles around in the bag, finds the picture and hands it to the genie.

The genie takes one look and says, 'So, do you want two lanes or four . . .?'

A dream came true for me the other day.
I partnered Stuart Appleby in the weekly club foursomes.

At least I think it was Stuart Appleby.

Because when he and I were beaten and we trudged off the eighteenth hole, he turned to me and said, 'If you're a golfer, then I'm Stuart Appleby . . .'

But, he must have really liked me, because at the end of the day, he also said that I was now on his hit list . . .

A guy named Joe finds himself in dire trouble.
His business has gone bust and he's in serious financial trouble. In fact, it looks like he will be unable to pay his golf subs and so won't be able to indulge in his greatest pleasure, golf.

He's so desperate that he decides to ask God for help.

He begins to pray, 'God, please help me. I've lost my business and if I don't get some money, I'm going to lose my house as well.

'If I lose my house, I won't have the money to pay my golf subs and then life will not be worth living.

'Please let me win the lotto.'

Lotto night comes and somebody else wins it. Joe again prays, 'God, please let me win the lotto! I've lost my business, my house and I'm going to lose my car as well and if I lose all those things I won't be able to afford my golf subs and then life won't be worth living.'

Lotto night comes and Joe still has no luck.

Once again, he prays, 'My God, why have you forsaken me? I've lost my business, my house and my car. My wife and children are starving and I can't pay my golf subs. Life is not worth living. I don't often ask you for help and I have always been a good servant to you. Please just let me win the lotto this one time so I can get my life back in order.'

Suddenly there is a blinding flash of light as the heavens open and Joe is confronted by the voice of God himself, 'Joe, meet me halfway on this one. Buy a lotto ticket.'

Don't think,' she says to her husband, 'That you are going to sneak off and play golf and leave me here to do all the work, cleaning up the kitchen.'

'Of course not,' says the husband. 'Golf is the furthest thing from my mind. Now would you please pass me the putter? Er, I mean butter . . .'

TV TRAUMA

WAYS TO ANNOY YOUR GOLFING HUSBAND WHEN THE MASTERS GOLF TOURNAMENT IS ON TV

1. Take the batteries out of all of the remote controls.
2. Show a sudden interest in every aspect of the game, especially have him define the laws of golf for you, many times.
3. Plug in a boom-box in the room and do your dance aerobics routine.
4. Decide it's time to dust the house, starting with a particularly good dusting of the TV set right at the first drive of the day.
5. Invite your mother over.
6. Get a magazine, sit in the room and read the articles out loud.

7. Hide the beer and snacks.
8. Come into the room every two minutes to complain about the television volume being too loud.
9. Choose a player and cheer loudly for him.
10. It's your night out with the girls . . . leave the kids home with him!

YOUNG GOLFERS

'L et me inform you, young man,' said the slow elderly golfer,
'I was playing this game before you were born.'

'That's all very well, but I'd be obliged if you would try to
finish it before you die.'

T wo young boys were spending the night at their old
grandparents.

At bedtime, the two boys kneeled down beside their beds to
say their prayers.

Suddenly, the youngest boy began praying at the top of his
lungs, 'I pray for a new set of golf clubs. I pray for a new golf
bag. I pray for a new VCR so I can watch golf videos.'

His older brother leans over, nudges his younger brother
and says, 'Why are you shouting your prayers? God isn't
deaf!'

The little brother replied, 'No, but Grandma sure is!'

L ittle Johnny is at the golf club trophy night because a
babysitter was not available. His parents tell him to be polite
and not to draw attention to himself.

An old golfer calls Little Johnny over to him and starts asking
about school, girlfriends and other stuff he can think of.

After a while, the old golfer notices that Little Johnny is
becoming bored with the conversation so he pulls out two
bills from his wallet to see if he can keep him interested—a
five and a 20 dollar bill.

He shows both bills to Little Johnny and tells him that he can keep any one he chooses.

Little Johnny reaches over and grabs the five dollar bill.

The old golfer, pretty surprised and upset about the unwise decision his grandchild made, pulls out another five dollar bill to see if it was a mistake.

Again, he tells Little Johnny to take one of the bills and keep it.

Little Johnny grabs the other five.

The old golfer again is surprised and upset.

He takes Little Johnny over to one of the uncles and shows him how dumb Little Johnny is in choosing the five over the 20.

The old golfer goes on and on showing every uncle and cousin and each time Little Johnny chooses the five over the 20.

The old golfer finally shows the stunt to the lad's dad.

The dad's quite surprised and walks off shaking his head.

A few hours later, dad walks up to Little Johnny and asks him if he now knows the difference between a five dollar bill and a 20.

'Of course I do,' answers Little Johnny. 'I did all along.'

'So why did you always choose the five over the 20?' asks dad.

Flipping through a stack of notes, Little Johnny, with a wide smile answers, 'Well dad, if I had chosen the first 20 dollar bill, do you think the old golfer would have played the same game 15 more times?'

It's the first day of school and the teacher thought she'd get to know the kids by asking them their name and what their father does for a living.

The first little girl says: 'My name is Mary and my daddy is a postman.'

The first little boy says: 'I'm Andy and my dad is a mechanic.'

Then one little boy says, looking quite ashamed: 'My name is Johnny and my father cleans toilets for a living.'

The teacher awkwardly and quickly changes the subject, but later in the school yard the teacher approaches Johnny privately and asks if it was really true that his Dad cleans toilets for a living, wanting to talk with him about his shame.

He blushed and said, 'No, I'm sorry. My dad is a professional golfer and I was just too embarrassed to say so . . .'

A young Scottish caddie and lass were sitting on a low stone wall, gazing across the small loch on the twelfth hole.

For several minutes they sat silently, holding hands.

Then finally the girl looked at the boy and said, 'A penny for your thoughts, Angus.'

'Well, uh, I was thinking, perhaps it's about time for a wee kiss.'

The girl blushed, then leaned over and kissed him lightly on the cheek.

Then he blushed.

The two turned once again to gaze out over the loch.

Minutes passed and the girl spoke again. 'Another penny for your thoughts, Angus.'

'Well, uh, I was thinking perhaps it's no about time for a wee cuddle.'

The girl blushed, then leaned over and cuddled him for a few seconds.

Then he blushed.

Then the two turned once again to gaze out over the loch.

After a while, she again said, 'Another penny for your thoughts, Angus.'

'Well, uh, I was thinking perhaps it's about time you let me put my hand on your leg.'

The girl blushed, then took his hand and put it on her knee. Then he blushed.

The two turned once again to gaze out over the loch before the girl spoke again.

'Another penny for your thoughts, Angus.'

The young man glanced down with a furled brow. 'Well, now,' he said, 'my thoughts are a wee bit more serious this time.'

'Really?' said the lass in a whisper, filled with anticipation.

'Aye,' said the lad, nodding.

The girl looked away in shyness, began to blush and bit her lip in anticipation of the ultimate request.

Then he said, 'Do ye nae think it's about time ye paid me the first three pennies?'

F ive young Scotsmen and five young Englishmen were travelling via train to have a golf weekend.

The Scots had their clubs and bags, but only one ticket between them.

Just before the conductor came through, all the Scots and their gear piled into the toilet stall at the back of the car.

As the conductor passed the stall, he knocked and called, 'Tickets, please!' and one of the Scots slid a ticket under the door.

It was punched, pushed back under the door and when it was safe all the Scots came out and took their seats.

The Englishmen who observed this were tremendously impressed by the Scots' ingenuity.

Next trip the Englishmen decided to try this themselves and purchased only one ticket.

They noticed that, oddly, the Scots had not purchased any tickets this time.

Anyway, again, just before the conductor came through, the

Scots piled into one of the toilet stalls, the Englishmen into the other.

Then one of the Scots leaned out, knocked on the Englishmen's stall and called 'Ticket, please!' When the ticket slid out under the door, he picked it up and quickly closed the door.

A n American tourist was playing golf in Scotland when he came to a hole with a fast flowing river running down the side of the fairway.

A young boy was sitting at the bank of the river and as the tourist hooked his drive, it hit the boy who fell into the river.

By the time the worried golfer arrived at the river bank, the boy was sinking into the deep water for the third time and was looking poorly.

The tourist immediately jumped into the river and after a real struggle managed to bring the boy to dry land where he quickly revived him.

He then brought the boy back to the clubhouse where he arranged for a taxi to take the boy home.

About an hour later a man arrived at the clubhouse and asked the pro, 'Could you tell me where the man is who saved my son?'

The pro replied, 'He's over in the hotel—check with the receptionist.'

The man then went to the hotel and asked the receptionist, 'Could you tell me where the man is who saved my son?'

'Yes, I'll call his room and ask him to come down,' was the reply.

A few minutes later the American tourist came down. The man asked him, 'Are you the man who saved my son?'

'Yes, I sure am,' was the reply.

'Well, would you have his cap . . .?'

Albert Einstein arrives at a College party and introduces himself to the first person he sees and asks, 'What is your IQ?' to which the man answers '241.'

'That is wonderful!' says Einstein. 'We will talk about the Grand Unification Theory and the mysteries of the Universe. We will have much to discuss!'

Next Einstein introduces himself to a woman and asks, 'What is your IQ?'

To which the lady answers, '144.'

'That is great!' responds Einstein. 'We can discuss politics and current affairs. We will have much to discuss!'

Einstein goes to another person and asks, 'What is your IQ?' to which the man answers, '51.'

Einstein quickly responds, 'How 'bout that Tiger Woods?'